HOW TO

UNSTOPPABLE CONFIDENCE

WITHIN YOURSELF

The Ultimate Guide to Building Inner Strength,
Unleashing Your Potential, Cultivating a Growth
Mindset, and Achieving Your Best Life

Lara J. Noble

derived from various sources. Please consult a licensed professional before attempting any techniques outlined in this book.

By reading this document, the reader agrees that under no circumstances is the author responsible for any losses, direct or indirect, that are incurred as a result of the use of the information contained within this document, including, but not limited to, errors, omissions, or inaccuracies.

Contents

INTRODUCTION

One important key to success is self-confidence. An important key to self-confidence is preparation. -Arthur Ashe

Growing up, I used to believe that people who come from financially privileged backgrounds have higher intelligence, are physically attractive, have a thriving social life, and are the only lucky ones likely to have great confidence in life. As I got exposed to many cultures and different people from across the world, I couldn't help but notice that that belief was rather flawed. Having all the above privileges does not guarantee that someone will grow up to be confident at all. What even astounded me more were statistics that were uncovered by a study conducted on some college students in the United States of America. This study suggested that over 70% of people attested that their career success was mainly a result of being very confident. 62% of students reported to be battling with anxiety due to a lack of confidence. As you may have also noticed, many people start to lose confidence drastically during their teenage years. To confirm this, a study determined that over 40% of girls in the United Kingdom experienced a significant decline in their confidence levels during their adolescent years. Over 63% of people reported that having imposter syndrome negatively impacted their confidence so much. In assessing the overall results of the study, it was determined that confidence is the biggest personality trait that determines how others perceive someone to be attractive. People with stunning confidence, even if their looks or intelligence is deemed as average, are considered to be more attractive and charismatic (Gitnux, 2023).

All the above statistics offer us a glimpse of the significance of mastering the incredible and unprecedented quality of being a confident person. Essentially, the idea is that, even if you are equipped with great talent and resources, without confidence, you are likely to live way below your potential and shy away from your potential greatness. The question is, even though we have seen countless evidence of the importance of confidence, why is it that we still tiptoe around confidence instead of grabbing it and just allowing ourselves to be fully immersed in it every day? What is it about the confidence that makes it so hard for many people to embody it and let it shine unapologetically?

The pain of seeing your dreams at a far distance, not because that's how it's meant to be but because you know that you are afraid, is unbearably excruciating. Knowing that many factors are impeding you from having the confidence to ferociously go after what you want can feel suffocating—hence the sleepless nights spent browsing websites about confidence and watching endless videos on how to develop lasting confidence. Sometimes, such searches give you a boost of hope and motivation, but your confidence can hit rock bottom in no time again as soon as you start feeling demotivated and fearful again. This cycle of intermittent patterns of confidence has led people to feel like true lasting confidence is unattainable. Many myths have been born from people's unpleasant experiences with trying to defeat a lack of confidence. These myths also start to be some of the hindering factors that block you from taking actions that will improve your confidence.

To get a better idea about what some of the common myths are on confidence, consider the following limiting beliefs most people reinforce in their mindset: the belief that confidence is most certainly always destroyed by negative critique, the idea that being our biggest critics will push us to have the confidence to reach our goals, the notion that a confident person is never afraid or insecure, and the paralyzing idea that you first need to be confident before you can achieve great things. This is just to mention a few of these crippling assumptions people hold onto, which become roadblocks in stopping them from doing things that will amplify their confidence even more.

Let's debunk the above myths together, shall we? Do you believe that all confident people you've met never receive negative criticism? Would you say they hardly ever struggle with anxiety, doubt, or fear? Do you think their successes only came after they first developed confidence? On the contrary, the opposite is actually true for all these myths. Many people who are confident develop the ability to accept critique with an open mind and see it as a learning tool instead of a weapon meant to attack them. Even if they do get malicious and malevolent comments, their confidence still prevails because what they believe about themselves is their primary truth and concern more than what others think or have to say.

Confident people hone the skill of developing firm assurance in themselves such that whatever comes from the external environment goes through a mental sifting stage whereby only what is productive is allowed to seep into their brains, while everything else they consider to be mere fluff is diplomatically ignored. And yes, you certainly do not have to wait to have confidence before deciding to go after your dreams. How it works is that doing what you are afraid or unsure of, that's actually how you grow to develop greater confidence. Automatically, that means that confident people allow themselves to fail because they embrace failure as an essential part of becoming a greater version of themselves. It is our experiences, our victories won when we acted out of courage even though trembling with fear inwardly that make someone develop unshakeable confidence.

The idea that you cannot be confident because of the wrong belief that your strengths, gifts, expertise, skills, and talents are finite only holds people back from living large. How can you possibly discover unlived versions of yourself when you allow your life to be limited by having a fixed mindset? The prospect of experiencing sides of yourself you may not know and a more fulfilling life only remains open when you determine to have a growth mindset as the standard of your reasoning and way of life.

What's even sadder is when you meet people who believe that the only time they will be confident is when they reach some perfect ideal they believe they should have first. This could be an ideal they have of how they should look, how much they should earn, where they should live, what sort of job they should have, the kind of car they should drive, and all sorts of materialist standards that are unreasonable parameters to draw out for themselves. From my life experiences, the most confident people I recall were actually people who were very aware of their flaws but what made them stand out is that they gracefully embraced their shortcomings and didn't emit an energy that suggested to others that they are pressurizing themselves to be perfect before they can accept who they are. You could tell that from simply accepting themselves and even adding humor when talking about their flaws, it made them very magnetic to others. The reason is simply that people can relate with you when you show that you aren't afraid to embrace your flaws. Yes, confident people don't spend hours harshly judging themselves and blowing all sorts of negative comments. Instead, they focus on the positive and highlight their strengths whilst making it clear that they are a work in progress when it comes to overcoming their flaws.

Confidence is incredibly attractive and yes, you certainly do not have to have it all figured out before you can start walking with your head held up high. What's likely stopping you from becoming a greater version of yourself is not the material resources you might have believed you need for you to have grounded confidence. All you need is simply a change in perspective. Realize that as you change the attitude you have toward yourself and strengthen the confidence you have in yourself, there is no limit to the amount of success and abundance you are guaranteed to attract.

You won't need to pay a cent to develop this unprecedented confidence in yourself. However, just like anything worth having hardly comes free of charge, there is indeed a price to pay. The good news is that that price is definitely within your budget, you can afford to pay it. All you have to do is to be resolute and commit to winning this race no matter how hard the grind gets. That price is called discipline. Without discipline, we can easily allow anything to run our lives. Mastering self-confidence will require you to be disciplined about no longer making room for excuses. It demands a commitment from you to no longer subscribe to old patterns of things that used to erode your confidence. Instead, all you have to do is to allow change to set in your life for good. To start this marvelous journey that will impact the rest of your life and well-being, let's dive into the first chapter and explore in depth what confidence is and how it all works.

CHAPTER 1

Understanding Confidence

*As soon as you trust yourself, you will know how to live. -
Johann Wolfgang von Goethe*

This magical word *confidence* has no doubt stirred the
mainstream media and is often spoken about literally
anywhere you go across this entire globe. One may wonder,
what is it about confidence which makes people so crazy
about it? What's even more important is how one can
develop confidence, since it seems not everyone is
inherently born with it and immediately just starts to rock it
as they navigate throughout the years in their lives. It is no
doubt that out of all the splendid and exquisite fashion in this
world, including that which is still to be designed,
confidence remains the number-one trait to clothe yourself
with. Its dazzling, mesmerizing, and magnetic effect always
draws people to whoever dares to wear that sought-after

apparel known as confidence. It is fair to consider confidence as one of the rarest and best qualities that anyone can ever possess. With confidence, you gain the ability to dream and move those dreams into reality. With confidence, you often get the answer "Yes," whereas others often get dismayed with the answer "No."

Confidence attracts so much success, adventure, and abundance in one's life that the prospect of continuing to live without it just seems so tragic and even morbid. Let's face it, we all tremendously need stunning confidence. Without it, we become familiar friends with mediocrity and life lived with sheer regret and sadness. To ensure that this will never become the reality you and I face, let's dive deep into unpacking what exactly confidence is and how to master it so well such that there won't be any need to fake it anymore. Yes, don't we all at some point fake it? I think if you are honest with yourself, you would admit that at some point, survival meant you had to fake it to make it. Nevertheless, let's close the curtains of that season, and open a new chapter of unlimited confidence. This is the only way you and I can live an abundant life full of great victories. Are you ready?

To address the basic question of what confidence is, it can be defined as having great conviction and faith in one's abilities to overcome any challenges and bravely take the necessary action needed. Confidence is the trust we have that we can achieve what we set out to do no matter how dire the obstacles on the way may seem to be. This explains why confidence is fundamental for excelling in any aspect of your life. It takes courage and trust to show up at work or in your relationships with your head held up high and expect others to give you what is due to you. Many people who look for life partners almost always find confidence as one of the most attractive traits anyone can ever have. The majority of jobs are always on the hunt for workers who exhibit unapologetic confidence. Friends and families find people who are confident among them to be rather more appealing to be around. Confident people easily attract large volumes of human traffic into their lives because human beings in general find confident people to be very refreshing and inspiring. It puts people at ease and in a great mood when you are confident. Do you remember how you felt the last time you were around someone who evidently appeared to be nervous and uncomfortable with themselves? Somehow being around people who feel awkward about themselves just makes it awkward for others too. This explains why people who lack confidence are often the ones chasing after others and the opposite is true. Confident people always seem to have such a great following of admirers, be it online or in person. It seems like confident people have such progressive lives that are characterized by goals being met and dreams being fulfilled sooner than the amount of time their counterparts tend to take.

If confidence is this impactful, surely it would be utter folly to procrastinate investing in learning more about how you can make it a permanent part of your identity and everyday life.

How Confidence Daily Impacts Your Relationships

Confidence allows one to have enriched life experiences. However, if you do not understand how to exhibit confidence, you would be short-changing yourself greatly. This is why this section will help you to solve that problem and ensure that you understand all the nuances in connection with having massive confidence. There are several components of confidence we will explore now.

Confident people trust themselves: People who are confident have a greater degree of self-trust. They believe in themselves and trust in their intuition and outlook on things. Even if they fail, they still do not allow those failures to erode their confidence or self-esteem. Have you ever seen people that seem to always check in first with others if what they want to do is okay? Sometimes it's wise to do so but at times this can indicate a lack of confidence in oneself. If you feel that other people's opinions and ideas are more trustworthy and valuable than yours then this alone can signify an apparent lack of self-confidence. When people notice that you second-guess yourself so much, they too start to doubt the credibility of your input and begin to lose confidence in you. To prevent this reality from unfolding in your interactions and life experiences, you can start to practice being more trusting of yourself. If you used to rely on others for making personal decisions, then you can start by trusting that you do have the wisdom and intelligence to make the right decisions for yourself. The more you develop your self-trust, the more your confidence will shine. Believing and trusting in yourself makes you charismatic and others start to find you magnetic. The more you trust yourself, the more you will have the courage to try new things, and this leads to constant and explosive growth in your life. Without self-trust, it's hard to have the tenacity and grit you need to create the most exciting and adventurous life you can possibly live. Self-trust allows you to move away from your comfort zone and reach out for new enriching opportunities.

Confident people tend to be more self-aware: Confident people tend to be very aware of their worth and abilities. They have a strong sense of personal identity which they are mindful of. This protects them from predatory characters who tend to take advantage of people's insecurities and blind spots. For example, you can hardly bring down someone who is confident through demeaning and insulting false comments. It's almost like many of the negative things people throw at them hit an invisible shield and never get to affect them at all. For you to also develop your self-awareness, mindfulness exercises can be helpful. This entails taking time to meditate on affirmations that reinforce in you the truth about your identities and capabilities. The more you become grounded in your truth and embrace your unique abilities, the more you start to reach out for the life you deserve. When you aren't unsure of your potential and what you are capable of, it makes you a hesitant person who is often either cynical or fearful of taking chances in life.

A great example to elaborate on the impact of lacking self-awareness is when someone is bullied. The bullies can plant in that person's mind the belief that they are weak and bound to live that difficult life of being jeered on and harassed by others. They can even make you feel like you deserve to be treated poorly. What's even more heartbreaking is when they reinforce in the person the idea that no one cares about them and so even if they report the bullying, nothing will change but things will only get worse. Instead of taking action to end the bullying, that negative indoctrination from others can lock the bullied victim in a cycle of constant abuse. What do you think would happen if the victim was aware of themselves and knew that they don't deserve to be treated poorly? If the victim believed that they had the ability to defend themselves one way or the other, it would short-circuit that abuse in no time.

The bullies' strengths prevail for as long as the victim remains unaware of their potential and self-worth. However, if the victim woke up to the fact that they are precious and no one deserves to be treated that way, it would stir great confidence in them which would enable them to either fight back or report the matter. Indeed, only when we are aware of how wonderful and powerful we are, would we cease settling for less.

Confident people have self-compassion: It is no secret that people who are confident treat themselves much better than those who aren't. They practice a greater degree of self-compassion and do not allow negative chatter to overtake their perception of themselves. Self-compassion is the ability to be able to treat yourself with kindness, empathy, understanding, patience, and respect despite your shortcomings. When you support and encourage instead of pulling yourself down, you lift up your spirit and open up your mind toward being more embracing of all the possibilities of a great life. However, when one's mind is inclined to self-loathing and harsh criticism, this paralyzes one's confidence and makes it hard to see and believe how you can improve things. Rumination is a terrible habit whereby we mull over our mistakes and flaws and start feeling like losers or inadequate for performing certain roles.

The great news is that you can free yourself from this behavior by being mindful of the monologue constantly happening in your head. Whenever you catch yourself being negative or giving yourself destructive criticism, it's always best to interrupt that thought pattern by refusing to dwell on any negativity and placing your focus rather on who you want to be. The more you focus on who you want to be, the less you will have time to reinforce the character you no longer want to be. It's just like how focusing on creating positive new habits instead of trying so hard to stop bad habits can gradually put an end to the negative habits.

For instance, when people are skiing, if you tell them not to focus on trees, the irony is that all they will start seeing and focusing on are trees. This increases the likelihood of them running into the trees they are now focusing on. That is why the key to skiing so well is to always focus on the path you want to take, that way you automatically avoid running into any obstacles. This is an important life lesson confident people master. They choose not to focus on their weaknesses by amplifying or talking about them. Rather, they make who they want to show up as the main focus. That way, they are left with more energy to inject into who they want to become and end up getting better and better with time. What makes people feel like they can't be compassionate for themselves is when they assume that they deserve to look down on themselves and believe that what their inner critic is saying is true. This means that all of that way of thinking has to be discarded if you want to overcome negativity and start treating yourself with love and compassion.

Confident people are articulate and freely express themselves: What makes us know if someone is confident upon casting our glance at them is when they express themselves well verbally and nonverbally. Self-expression is not just limited to what you say with your words. It also encompasses how you live, how you carry yourself, and how you go after your dreams, and the challenges you face. Being candid and assertive is one of the core aspects of being good at expressing yourself. Confident people believe that their opinion matters and this makes them not withdraw their ideas from others. They express themselves unapologetically and with so much ease that it mesmerizes their listeners into wanting to hear even more from them. They voice out their viewpoints not only verbally but also with supporting gestures. Self-advocacy is also an integral part of how they successfully navigate their interpersonal engagements. Self-expression also entails being able to be your unique self without feeling the need to conform to other people's expectations.

When you are confident, you value what you believe in and live a life that respects your values and standards. Sometimes you can see that someone is great at how they express themselves through how they dress, what they choose to settle for, and how they teach people to treat them. If you want to become better at expressing yourself, it's important to practice not sidelining your thoughts and how you feel. You should never allow other people to talk over you and disregard what you have to say. Take time to know who you are and what matters to you, then start living a life true to that. If you don't agree with something, start practicing assertively stating your stance. The more we express ourselves and stop hiding who we really are, the more fulfilling our lives will start to feel. Self-expression also helps us to connect deeply with others and build long-lasting relationships. The world always has a way of making room for someone who dares to believe that they are worth taking up space and sharing their contribution. Start to practice speaking your mind more but first reflect on how you can sharpen your communication skills so that when you do express yourself, your words and actions are impactful.

How do all these components of self-confidence affect your daily life and relationships? Self-trust is an extremely crucial aspect of who we all need to be because if you don't trust your abilities and doubt yourself, you will hardly grow. You start to have a fixed mindset and resist change and opportunities for growth. However, with self-trust, you always maintain the belief that no matter what life will throw at you, there is always a way you will overcome the trials. This makes you expose yourself to opportunities that make you a better person. When you are self-aware, your relationships become healthier because you will be able to keep toxic behaviors that hurt others at bay. However, people who lack awareness keep hurting others, including themselves. If you aren't aware that you are a superb human being who has the potential to be many things in this life and not just one thing, you become invincible, the world starts to be your stage. There is no end to the different skills you can acquire and use to better your life and the lives of others. Let's say you believe you are only good at dancing; this might make you miss out on many other things you could potentially be good at such as sports, singing, and other professions.

Being self-aware helps us to remember that we are not just limited to the version of ourselves we have known up until now. We are reminded of many of the other opportunities life has in store for us which we can certainly juggle too. This makes us live an enriched life full of variety and adventure. When we are compassionate for ourselves, we treat ourselves in a beautiful way which also inspires others to see us in the same light. Once others see us in a positive light, our relationships with them start to soar. Being insecure makes it hard to develop healthy relationships because your way of receiving and giving love might have toxic elements to it. For example, insecure people sometimes threaten others or act passive-aggressively when they want to receive love. This can strain relationships and fill your life with stress and anxiety.

On the other hand, confident people express themselves clearly and directly voice their concerns. This makes it easier for others to know how they can meet their needs better. Generally, confident people are happier. When you are happy, it makes others want to be around you since our moods are affected by the attitudes other people around us display. This happiness comes from training your mind to view life from a positive instead of a negative outlook. If we have a positive view of ourselves, it makes us have high self-esteem which also leads to relationship success because people tend to gravitate toward people with high self-esteem. For us to build amazing lives, we have to pursue confidence and escape the urge to settle for less. Confidence is attractive, it makes your life attract so much abundance and success. Every aspect of our lives is impacted by confidence; this is why we have every element of it so that you can be fully equipped to be confident and live a full life with no regrets.

The Impactful Connection Between Confidence, Gratitude, and High Self-Esteem

Have you ever noticed something really special about most confident people? They have the ability to focus so much on their strengths and what's going well for them that there is hardly any room for dwelling on the negative aspects of their lives. This way of thinking only makes them have compounded success because when you have a grateful heart it makes you have an attractive attitude. Everyone loves being around people who are thankful and not whiners and complainers. What makes people fall into the habit of constantly complaining and feeling dissatisfied with their lives is the habit of dwelling on what they don't have. It's okay to be mindful of what we still need to achieve but if we do this so much to the extent that we forget to be thankful for what we already have, it can throw us into a toxic pattern of living. To elaborate more on this point, let's say you have always wanted to have a great life partner. One day you suddenly meet that person and feel so thankful for finally meeting the love of your life. Then as the relationship progresses, you start to notice many things your partner isn't doing for you yet which you want them to do. Instead of inspiring them to do more of those things for you by showing them an appreciation for what they are already doing so far, you jump into a pattern of constantly complaining and

25

criticizing them. Before long, your partner can start to feel under-appreciated and unmotivated to keep trying to meet your needs because for as long as they don't perfectly do everything you want, you always complain and focus on the one or two things they haven't done yet. This can be very damaging to relationships and even make you risk losing a great person you could have possibly built a strong lifelong relationship with if only you were patient and grateful for the small steps you are taking.

To be a grateful person we have to direct our minds toward being thankful for how far we have come so far. Show appreciation to yourself and others for all the victories you have had up until now. Don't let what you don't have yet make you lose your joy in the present and turn you into a chronic complainer.

When you are grateful for all you have and can do, it inspires you to take more chances in life and keep progressing. Think about how many obstacles and limitations you have overcome up until now. Just remembering all the good things you managed to achieve so far can help you to have faith in yourself and develop massive confidence. You will know that you have all it takes to win your present battles just as you managed to overcome your past battles.

Without gratitude, what's magnified are always your weaknesses and limitations. Once this is all that's dominating your thinking, your confidence is eroded as you become less connected to your strengths. Up until now, we might have been addicted to an ungrateful and cynical way of life on the assumption that we are being realists, but it's time that addiction is broken before it causes more harm. Life is about constant growth. There is never a time when you will feel like you have become everything you were meant to be because each day that dawns gives you a new chance to grow beyond where you are now. This is why we have to learn to be content and happy with our step-by-step success. We have to learn to celebrate and embrace where we are now. This makes you a confident person since you will no longer be using the wrong scale to weigh how successful you are. True success is being able to live a grateful life and bring light and joy to yourself and others. What we achieve makes us happy and gives us more confidence in ourselves. However, we still have to develop sustainable confidence from just being grateful for being who we are... having the gift of life. If your worth and confidence are only based on the material possessions you have, you cannot develop lasting confidence because there is always more to achieve which can make you feel insecure with your level of achievement for now. This is why we have to rather base our confidence on knowing and being grateful for who we are as human beings. Babies come into this world with nothing, but just consider how confident they are! Their confidence is not confined to what they possess but in just knowing that they are precious and worthy of love. We need to go back to this pure way of thinking and remember that our confidence should always be based on our true identity and worth as human beings. This makes you live a grateful life and no longer let your happiness be controlled by what you have or don't have.

Remember that we can hardly get what we want by being negative, rather, the quickest way to get what we need is by learning to appreciate and treat well what we already have. Consider turning over a green leaf and committing to live a life free from any form of negativity, especially the habit of giving yourself and others destructive criticism. When tempted to complain, rather choose to express your gratitude for all the things already going well for you. This makes you have such a pleasant and beautiful personality others will love being around. This also improves your confidence and self-belief as you start to realize how amazing your life already is as where you are now.

Reflection on Your Confidence Journey So Far

Now let's think about how you would describe yourself when it comes to confidence. Would you say you live most of your days showing up as a confident person? What are the common habits you repeatedly do that make you exude a lack of confidence and bring you down? What can you do to become a more confident person? When was the last time you felt very confident and what inspired that confidence? What more can you do so that you can strengthen your confidence muscles? Vividly imagine what you would be like if your confidence wasn't limited. Here are a few tips and reminders to help you reframe your mindset so that you embody confidence more:

- Confident people do not tolerate negativity either from themselves or others.

- Confident people speak in a candid manner, respectfully, and choose the right time to say things.

- To be confident, there is a need to stop questioning and doubting yourself but rather only focus on your strengths.

- Gracefully accepting constructive feedback and not being defensive is a sign of confidence and maturity.

- Confident people allow themselves to make mistakes without ending up self-loathing and punishing themselves. They know that mistakes are an essential part of growing and value the process.

- Confident people don't use other people's success as a benchmark to measure their own worth. They know that they are running their unique race and focus on improving how they were yesterday.

- Confident people express themselves freely, enjoy their lives, and appreciate what they have.

Having explored all the critical elements of confidence, undoubtedly you now know that this is definitely a quality you can master in no time. Once the battle is won in the mind, there is nothing that can stop you from building up your self-confidence and living your life with more excellence than before. Now it's time we have a look at how you can embrace your unique self and develop confidence in the real you.

CHAPTER 2

Embrace Your Unique Self

We are not in control, principles control. We control our actions, but the consequences that flow from these actions are controlled by our principles. -Stephen R. Covey

Knowing who you are and what makes you distinctly unique helps you to navigate through life with confidence and well-established personal boundaries that protect what matters most to you. Identifying what you consider as the most important personality attributes and behaviors helps you to know the kind of values which resonate the best with you. Values are essentially the moral codes and standards we set for ourselves that govern how we interact with our world. Someone who has well-established values and keeps upgrading themselves to be a better person is bound to attract success and great progress in almost every aspect of their lives. Your values make up who you are and determine the quality of life you will attract for yourself. If you don't have set values you are aware of, don't worry at all. This chapter will help you to understand how you can establish the best values which align with the goals you wish to achieve. We will also have a deep dive into exploring how you can be mindful of all the things that make up who you are and use that to the best of your abilities. Understanding what your strengths and weaknesses are helps you to amplify those good traits and find a way to overcome your limitations. Overall, this self-introspection journey will help you to leverage all your abilities and harness your talents and skill sets to create the life you wish to live.

The personal values people have are derived from the kind of upbringing they have and what they eventually choose for themselves when they come of age. This means that most of the things you may deem as important to you are probably influenced by how you grew up and the kind of environment and cultural standards you were exposed to. As you grow older, it is important to start evaluating those standards and check if they align with what you personally believe and want to identify with. This is when you have to start intentionally establishing the list of values that will best represent who you are and who you want to become. When personal values are not set, it is very easy for others to take advantage of you or for you to settle for a life below what you are capable of creating for yourself. Personal values are key when creating and maintaining boundaries and drawing the parameters around what you will accept and what you will not condone. There are a number of ways you can establish your personal values. Think about what matters most to you and that will help you to know the values you have to uphold in order to advocate for your dreams and the quality of life you want. Below are examples of values and why you may consider choosing any of them to be your primary standards.

- **Patience:** It takes time to achieve what you want the right way. Exercising patience as your top value can help you to be someone who makes thoughtful decisions instead of rushed decisions. It can mean that when tempted to choose the easy way out or give in to instant gratification, you choose to be someone who works hard instead for the sustainable success of temporal fleeting pleasures.

- **Forgiveness:** Forgiveness is a quality you can embody in your nature by choosing to let go of resentment, bitterness, and any kinds of negative feelings toward yourself and others. It means that when tempted to hold grudges, you choose instead to be someone who exercises empathy and compassion. You prioritize harmony and do whatever it takes to leave peacefully with yourself and others.

- **Kindness:** You can choose to embody kindness as one of your core values. This means that you decide to treat others with love and consideration instead of only being consumed with what only matters to you. Kindness is a beautiful quality that helps you to emit positive energy wherever you go. Being that good-hearted can help you to also be the kind of person others feel at ease around and gravitate toward.

- **Gratitude:** Being a grateful person makes you so pleasant to be around. This means in every situation, you choose to focus on the good in it and as you work toward your goals, you don't let that stop you from appreciating what you already have.

- **Excellence:** Excellence has to do with the quality of work we choose to put in and how we do things. Being someone who always delivers quality work and upholds an excellent work ethic does not automatically happen. Without being intentional, you can easily be someone who settles for mediocre things. That means choosing to make excellence your core value requires you to commit to a life of competence and high standards.

- **Consistency:** It's easy to do something once or twice, but to continue to show up as you wish to every day and faithfully complete your goals requires great willpower. Making consistency one of your core values helps you to have ongoing progress and success.

- **Trustworthiness:** When you choose to be trustworthy, it means in everything you do, you strive to maintain honesty and loyalty. Being trustworthy makes people find you reliable. You can always count on someone who upholds this quality as their core value. Their words are seldom ever empty words.

- **Faith:** Faith can be considered a core value since it can shape your behaviors and mentality. Being someone of faith means that even though you may not have all the answers figured out or means to do something, you still go ahead to do it, trusting that everything will ultimately work out well. Having a growth mindset requires you to have faith since you would have to trust in a version of yourself you might not have seen yet. Faith brings us closer to our dreams yet to be tangible realities.

Apart from the above-listed examples of some values you can think about having, there are still many others you can contemplate about. Examples of these include determination, fairness, friendships, authenticity, boldness, learning, adventure, openness, fame, achievement, beauty, curiosity, happiness, and so on.

Among all the above values discussed, which ones do you feel best to describe you? If you were to unleash your full potential, which values would you like to exercise more? Are there any other values you can think of not listed above that resonate best with you? What can you do each day to reinforce those values in your life? What hinders you from embodying most of the values you wish to have? These are the reflective questions you may ask yourself so that you can introspect where you stand and decide on what works best for you.

Your values help you to be aware of how to conduct yourself so that you can achieve the best possible outcomes you desire. They define you and show others who you are. When practiced often, they help you gain credibility and trust. To attain any goals and dreams, it's necessary to have a character that supports your pursuits. Values help you to show up as you ought to and also impact your confidence level. For instance, when you know and believe that friendship is your core value, you would be less likely to hesitate to reach out to others and open up yourself for new possible friendships. It gives you the drive and confidence you need to create a life with friends. Without values, it's hard for us to be grounded and understood by others.

Embrace Your Unique Qualities With Confidence

A life lived by trying to be who you are not can be considered a sad tale. This is because everyone is created with special and unique differences that if embraced and appreciated, bring so much significance. When we try to live our lives copying and pasting everything or anything we see around us, we can run the risk of straying further away from our true selves. With the powerful influence of social media in these modern days, there are always temptations to conform to trends, and what seems to be socially hyped at any given time. While this can make you gain temporal approval from others, you may lose the approval of someone who should matter the most–you. We sacrifice our worth when we abandon who we truly are. Even worse, we lose so much when we blindly go through life without deeply comprehending who we really arc and what makes us our unique selves.

Knowing yourself and gracefully accepting who you are helps you to love and treat yourself as best as possible. What makes you who you are is your weaknesses and strengths put together. That means to love yourself well, you have to know how to handle both your weaknesses and strengths. But before even jumping to that step, first, you would need to know who you really are. Your own knowledge based on what you think and what you went through is very fundamental. What can be helpful as well as asking your friends and family about yourself.

Take time to gather honest opinions from people who decently know you. How we perceive ourselves is seldom how others perceive us. Being open to knowing how others perceive us can help with making us aware of our blind spots and more aspects of ourselves. Taking personality tests can also help you to get a hang of your main personality attributes and most of the tests also provide advice on things you can do to overcome your weakness. Take some time to think about your entire character and also script all the ideas that come to your mind. As you become aware of your weaknesses, realize that it's a privilege and great advantage to even be aware of yourself. By practicing the growth mindset, you can start to empower and upskill yourself more. Facing your weaknesses is never a pleasant feat but focusing on the beauty you will achieve once all those weaknesses are dealt with can help you to have the strength to overcome them. Remind yourself why you are working on yourself because this is how you can love yourself truly.

The less you judge yourself and unapologetically allow yourself to "just be," the more others will start to gravitate toward you. People love other people who are comfortable in their skin and lovingly embrace themselves. Thus, start to confidently express yourself without holding back who you really are. It is far better to be loved for who you truly are than to act like someone you aren't each day.

The Beauty of Practicing Self-Acceptance

One of the biggest and most integral steps to take when embracing who you are is to learn to accept yourself. The sad reality about life is that when you do not love and accept yourself, others feel that energy and also start to lose faith in you. Chances are most of your life experiences will be filled with a lot of rejection. This is because by not accepting yourself, you are essentially rejecting yourself. When you do that, you start to also attract rejection based on how the law of attraction works. Self-acceptance is the answer to healing from the pain of loneliness and self-loathing.

Our daily lives are greatly impacted by the way we treat ourselves. When you embrace self-acceptance, it helps you to have the courage to ask for help when you need it, which ultimately allows you to keep growing. Accepting yourself also means not hiding away from your talents and calling. It is exercising your willpower to overcome challenges and doing whatever it takes to shine your light each day. By no means would you ever settle for the comfort zone when you know that there is so much in you yet to be unearthed and used to better the world around you? Our lives start to feel fake and unsettling when we shy away from the impulse to thrive we all often have. There are a number of things you can do to practice being more accepting of yourself. These include

- Refraining from unhealthy comparisons of yourself with others.

- Setting and maintaining clear healthy boundaries even when it's hard to do so.

- Silencing your inner critic and speaking more compassionately and kindly to yourself.

- Forgiving and not punishing yourself for what you did wrong. Rather just focus on self-improvement.

- Advocating for your values and never feeling the need to abandon them just to get validation from others.

- Practicing mindfulness to help you be more conscious of your daily habits and how to constantly improve.

- Treating yourself with love, respect, and utmost kindness.

- Seeking help to overcome any challenges and weaknesses you may be struggling with on your own.

- Keeping a journal of your life and writing down all the goals about what matters to you.

- Not standing in the way of achieving your fullest potential.

The only way we can build sincere relationships with ourselves and others is when we start showing up as our authentic selves. Without true self-acceptance, no amount of external achievements we make can fill the emptiness we might end up experiencing for years. You are beautiful and special; believe that and act like you do. Even if others don't, don't let that deter you from continually having confidence in yourself. Soon enough, other people catch up and also start to see us in a positive light. Dare to live a true life as who you are and continue to explore more upgraded versions of yourself as you grow. There is no limit to the amount of success you can attain once you start to believe in yourself without holding back. Now let's dive into the next chapter to explore ways in which you can unleash your inner strength and move forward to greater heights you know well enough that are awaiting you.

CHAPTER 3

Unlocking Inner Strength

The oak fought the wind and was broken, the willow bent when it must and survived. -Robert Jordan, the Fires of Heaven

Life has a way of unearthing so much about ourselves that we may never have known before. Usually, most lessons we acquire are learned during times of turbulence and adversity. It is only when life hits us hard that we come face to face with the reality of how strong we are. It is they who view these times as precious opportunities for growth and evolution who tend to get the most and the best out of situations that could have potentially broken them. Confidence is an enormously powerful attribute that is seldom acquired by theoretically learning confidence lessons. It is when you go through various challenges and choose to apply wisdom and good judgment in those situations that your confidence starts to grow.

As you face battles you never thought you could have ever managed to overcome, your confidence starts to grow. Each small battle won paves the way for you to win bigger battles because every step you take in moving forward and fighting for what you believe in helps you to realize the incredible amount of inner strength you have that may have been lying dormant. Having that said, I have seen throughout my life experiences how most strong people come from challenging backgrounds, and tend to have faced so many battles, and through those battles, they evolved into becoming the strong individuals we now see. In essence, this means that some setbacks we may view as terrible things are actually blessings and great opportunities in disguise for massive growth and unleashing the inner strength in you.

Let's consider how rocks are formed; what makes them so sturdy and strong? It is evidently their formation process. Rocks are formed under intense pressure underground and then emerge to the surface with time due to elements of the weather such as wind and water. Similarly, we too also go through a similar character formation process of being built into a strong individual by undergoing so many trials and hardships. Thereafter, certain things in our lives have to prevail to help us also submerge from hiding our inner strength. These "elements of the weather in our lives which push us up to the surface and make us have no choice but to shine our true beauty and strength"... can be considered to be

44

all those times when you felt tested and tried. It is the times when you were faced with opportunities that demanded you to step up and show up. It is the times that drove you to fight for your goals and as you started doing so, you realized with time that you are more powerful than you ever imagined. For instance, babies can never know that they are capable of walking and running unless they give up their comfort and embrace the challenge of learning how to crawl and eventually walk on their own. They have to endure the hardships of falling multiple times and the uncertainty of knowing whether they will make it or not. Without embracing that stage and taking on the challenge of learning to do what they have never done before, they would never be able to experience the joy and freedom of being able to freely move from place to place whenever they wish to on their own two feet. As they start walking slowly, their confidence starts to mount up, and each step they take helps them realize that they have the strength to make it. This strength is *only* ascertained the moment they embrace the struggle and take up the challenge of becoming more than they were before. Similarly, this is also how we ought to be. You might look at yourself in the mirror today and assume that what you know about yourself is all there is to know and your strength is limited to your current perception of how strong you are. However, the truth about how much you are capable of taking and how far you can go in life is only revealed when you actually take on life challenges bravely and allow yourself to be in a position of uncertainty and possibly failing.

When we fear failure so much that we end up shunning so many opportunities to expand ourselves, there is hardly any hope left for discovering greater versions of ourselves we potentially can be. Everyone is born with the unique ability to do something significant and helpful to humanity. However, you may never know for sure if you truly have those abilities unless you try to do something new. When you do jump into the unknown and start exploring various lengths you can come to, it is of great importance to always remember that just because you fail in the process in one way or the other doesn't mean you don't have everything it takes to make it. Consider how athletes are trained; not all of them automatically start being the greatest Olympian champions we see in the limelight. They all have a story about where they began. They started somewhere. It could have been with winning a 100-meter race, then they decide to try out the 200-meter race after some time. As they kept mastering the craft of how to run longer distances as fast as possible, some of the athletes started taking on greater challenges such as running 400 or 800-meter races and in some marathon races, even way more kilometers.

What happened? With each race they won, it helped them gain confidence in their abilities even more. They learned that they have the competence and perseverance it takes to withstand greater goals. Even with each defeat they would face, they also learn a lot about themselves. One of those lessons could be that they are fit enough to endure long distances and win the race. This realization becomes the feedback they need in order to prepare better and try again. Similarly, we too have to allow ourselves to embody this growth mindset if we are serious about fully comprehending how powerful we are. There is no dream too high to set for yourself if you are willing to put in the work and unleash the inner strength lying dormant.

Now let's consider the different aspects of what being with resilience entails. Someone of great strength is a person who has resilience and is able to stand their ground and not regress when times get tough. Without resilience, when storms and winds come, they just sweep us away. However, for people with resilience, when winds blow, they become like the trees, which don't break but rather harness that wind to become stronger than ever before. The only way you can know how powerful you are is if you are willing to take the heat that comes with various forms of adversity and pursue success. Success is absolutely an uncomfortable goal to pursue. It requires you to have discipline, determination, confidence, connections, strong willpower, endurance, competence, perseverance, character, and self-control, and to be able to consistently contribute your share of input in the various aspects of your life.

Perhaps you may feel like I don't have most of the qualities I just listed above and thus why bother to even believe that I can be successful? The good news is that there is no need to give in to that thought or feeling because you can certainly achieve success starting from where you are now. The whole point is for you to realize that you have the inner strength to build all those qualities. Nevertheless, the only way you can see that for yourself is if you practically embrace the struggle and make a resolute decision to start exercising those qualities as much as you can every single day. As humans, we are created with the ability to grow and experience greater dimensions of who we can be. All this depends on you. You can choose to either remain the same person you have always been for years or dare to embrace the pain of change—as long as it yields you better results. If you can pick your battles wisely and choose to embrace the pursuit of your higher self, failure only becomes a temporary experience instead of being an on-going undesirable pattern in your life. Any so-called defeat you face will never be permanent if you make progress your main objective. Failure just becomes a temporary lesson to equip you to do better next time.

Being a confident person requires you to build up your resilience muscles. That means that there is a strong need to have great coping skills that can help you to have bounce-back power when life brings you down. Without resilience, it's easy to turn back at any moment and give up believing in yourself. Considering the examples of athletes we discussed earlier, it is only through resilience that they eventually manage to run greater races and win them. It's hard to wake up early and regularly practice. Most people seldom ever enjoy the strenuous things they have to do in order to get where they need to be. However, what helps them to accept the grind and put in the work is being able to see beyond the pain of what they may be presently going through. If you can make where you are going the main focus, there is no amount of sacrifice you will deny yourself because you would be fully aware that every ounce of work you put in is worth it and will pay off extremely well in a matter of time. When we are resilient, we become strong in the face of opposition or discouragement. For instance, you might share your lofty goals for your life with someone and also have a positive self-concept. But other people who hear your outlook about yourself might not agree with you and start saying or doing mean things to plant self-doubt in you. Being resilient means you would be able to block all those negative narratives and just focus on the truth you know about yourself. Resilience gives you the ability to ignore or simply ward off any form of negativity in your way. It helps you to be resourceful and adaptive. When things get hard, instead of saying you aren't able to make it anymore, your mind naturally gravitates toward thinking of ways to make things work regardless of how dire the situation may seem.

Even if you are a confident person already, you will still face naysayers and things that try to pull you back. This is why you have to protect your confidence by being firmly grounded in your true identity and nurturing many other attributes that will also complement your confidence. Let's dive into the next section to delineate various ways in which you can build massive resilience in your character.

Tips on Building Resilience

To help you foster greater resilience, here are suggested strategies that you can graft into your lifestyle:

- **Effective communication:** Things can get very overwhelming and unbearable when we keep our worries pent up inside. Other people can only show up for us in ways we expect them to if we learn to effectively communicate our needs. This means that you have to find the best time possible to assertively and respectfully convey your concerns. The more others understand you better, the better they will be able to support you, which helps you to have the strength to maintain composure and keep going.

- **Have a purpose you are passionate about**: It's hard to stick through something when you barely understand why you are doing it and, in some cases, don't even care about it. Thus, to foster greater resilience, pursue what you are passionate about. It has to be something that complements who you want to be and the life you wish to create for yourself. We tend to have greater patience and resilience when we know that we are fighting for our true destiny.

- **Self-awareness:** When we are blind to our weaknesses and limitations, they can easily trip us when we least expect them. Take some time to understand what your weaknesses are so that you can counteract them before they get in the way of your progress and success.

- **Healthy coping skills:** What hinders people from being resilient is when they fail to adopt effective coping strategies in the midst of hardships. Think about ways you can deal with stress in an effective way. When stressed, it's hard to control our emotions. When these emotions become overwhelming, it can easily lead us into throwing in the towel. This is why practicing mindfulness, breathing exercises, confiding in loved ones, and doing any stress-relieving activities that won't jeopardize your success should be part of your coping mechanisms.

- **Self-care:** The more you look after yourself and ensure that you are in a good place mentally and physically, the less you will be prone to stumbling into needless failures. When we shower ourselves with love and endless compassion, this nurtures our confidence and creates an atmosphere supportive of continual growth.

- There are, of course, many other ways you can exercise your resilience muscles, including learning new ways of doing things more efficiently. One of the other primary enemies of progress is fear and anxiety. Fears can make you forget how powerful you are; this is why we have to unpack ways you can overcome it so that your life is not impeded from moving forward.

How to Overcome Your Fears and Anxieties So That You Can Start Implementing Your Goals

Being slothful, making countless excuses, procrastinating, and playing small are all signs and symptoms of fear and anxiety. When we are afraid and filled with anxiety, it makes it hard to believe that we are capable of winning whatever challenge we might be facing. This leads to complacency and stagnation, as no action is taken in advancing forward with our goals. People struggle with various kinds of fears such as fear of the unknown, fear of failure, failure of success, and even fear of knowing the truth.

To overcome fear, there are a number of things you can do consistently. The most important thing to recognize is that fear is not a true indication of reality. Fears spurn from the things we imagine in our heads, most of which are usually not true. We create all sorts of conclusions of how things will unfold if we do something and those outcomes can make it hard for us to even want to try anything new. Therefore, to overcome fear, it is expedient to learn to separate an imagined reality from the objective reality right in front of you. The objective truth is that you can never know if you really can't do something unless you try. The imagined reality is that if you do try out new things, chances are you will fail and everyone will look down on you. Thus, being rational and learning to take action regardless of how you feel or what you already concluded will happen can help to short-circuit the limitations that fear imposes on you.

Other ways to overcome fear include setting small goals and maintaining consistency in achieving them. Over time, those small goals become a mountain of accomplishments you made through dedication and hard work. You can also make fear work to the best of your interests by using it as a motivating factor. The fact that you feel afraid should be a sign to you that something is worth pursuing. So instead of seeing it as a cue to give up, you can use it as a tool to get yourself ready for action.

Having a growth mindset helps you to accept temporal defeat as part of the growth process. When we have a fixed mindset, fear takes hold of us. However, with a growth mindset, you choose to focus more on what you can achieve instead of your current limitations. You get excited about how your skills will improve through the experiences you will face instead of being ashamed and afraid of showing your weaknesses. A growth mindset allows you to no longer hide your fears, but rather identify and expose them so that you can get constructive feedback on ways to overcome them. Assuming that your strength, confidence, and abilities are static and can never be improved makes it hard to unleash your fullest potential. It also makes it impossible to live outside the box you would have created for yourself.

To develop a growth mindset, take time to review how other people grow. Most people grow because they allow themselves to fail, laugh at themselves, and adopt a positive mentality about things. Notice how the successful people around you keep progressing. As you observe their patterns, you will see that they keep venturing for new goals and pushing themselves. Likewise, if you also imitate their ways, and divorce the unhealthy addiction to certainty which stops you from diving into the unknown, there is no limit to the level of success you will attain.

Take on challenges, dare to explore, and make mistakes! That's how education and growth transpires.

The Importance of Motivating Yourself and Staying Inspired

Motivation is what will keep you showing up each day. It's hard to run after your goals when you feel drained, negative, and unmotivated. Waiting for others to motivate you can also place you in a compromised position where you can end up delaying your progress because you can never control when people choose to show up for you. This is why having a strong framework for motivating yourself and staying inspired will help you to get things done and not fall into slothful ways.

A key way to remain motivated is to always be in touch with the main reasons why you chose to do something. When you get carried away by the motions and lose touch with the reason why you even committed to a journey of bettering yourself, you can end up burning out in no time.

To prevent this from happening, take time to think about why you are doing what you are doing. Visualize and even dream about what you are striving to attain as much as possible. Picture where you are going and how you could be. Think about what you will lose if you decide to settle for less. All these things will help you to awaken your zeal and tenacity and foster resilience in you. As you motivate yourself, keep finding more ways to motivate yourself because doing the same things all the time when you feel demotivated might eventually stop working as the body would have gotten so used to that. It's like how exercises work: If you keep doing the same exercise over and over again without alternating with others, the body eventually stops responding the same way. Allow your imagination to take you to places and new ideas of ways you can keep your spirit inspired. Your motivation also motivates others, since we are beings who naturally feed off of each other's energy.

Your inner strength is fully unveiled the more you allow yourself to embrace different experiences. You are powerful beyond what you believe about yourself. Your inner strength is like a fountain that never dries out; use it! Now that we have looked into your inner strength, let's explore ways you can also make your outward features a superpower for you.

CHAPTER 4

Enhance Your Outer Beauty

Beauty is how you feel inside and it reflects in your eyes. - Sophia Loren

Beauty encompasses how we look inside and out. There is no doubt that while our inner beauty matters more than anything, our outward beauty also plays a great role in impacting our confidence levels. How you value and feel about yourself determines your self-esteem which also plays a great role in influencing your confidence levels. When we feel great about our outward appearance, it directly makes us confident and more accepting of ourselves. It is rare to see someone who believes in their beauty feeling ashamed of themselves. Rather, people who have a healthy body image and self-esteem turn out to be more confident and prouder of themselves. Confidence should never be mistaken for arrogance. Arrogance is when you have an unhealthy sense of self-importance which makes you behave in ways that

58

aren't noble and respectful, especially toward others. On the other hand, confidence is being sure of your competence and having faith in your abilities. Improving your physical appearance can help you improve your self-esteem and develop a better personal concept.

Naturally, as human beings, we are inclined to judge people based on how they look and the way we treat them will also correspond with our perception of them. For instance, I'm sure you've once noticed the way people take you seriously when you are dressed well. On the other hand, people can either look down on you or just sideline you when you aren't dressed well. Furthermore, when you feel like your outward appearance is average, it also makes you behave in ways in tandem with that belief that you are average-looking. One of the common ways we see this is when people settle for relationship partners who they consider as not too outside their league. All interpersonal relationships are affected by how confident you are. People find you more attractive and charismatic when you are someone with a positive self-image and self-esteem.

The importance of having a great outward appearance is also seen in the corporate world. When engaging with work colleagues or going to an interview, your success and likability are also determined by how put-together you look outwardly. Employers and co-workers love working with someone they perceive as confident because confidence is usually linked to competence as well.

When it comes to physical beauty, there is no set standard of how you ought to look for you to be considered as the ultimate definition of what being beautiful entails. It is always a subjective and relative matter. Regardless of what you look like, if you do not believe in yourself and love how you are then it's hard for you or others to see you as beautiful. This goes to show us the importance of being mindful about how we view ourselves. You could have a fit body, amazing smile, and great personality, but still fail to have a positive self-image. The danger of this is that in a matter of time, others also start to see you through your own negative lenses and second-guess their initial impression of you. When we think very poorly of ourselves, it makes us emit very negative energy that makes it hard for us to be confident or for others to have confidence in us.

There are many ways people treat their bodies in unkind ways. This includes dressing shabbily, not practicing good hygiene, eating unhealthy foods and drinks, depriving yourself of sleep, saying mean comments about your body, being ashamed of how you look, and always trying to cover up even when it's not necessary.

Instead of reinforcing those unhealthy ways of treating yourself, it's better to start practicing self-love and self-care more so that you can develop a better relationship with your body. What usually gets in the way of developing a positive body image is when we use unfair standards to compare ourselves to others. For instance, nowadays there are so many filters and plastic surgery options to alter the way bodies look. If you compare your body with those unrealistic images of how people are supposedly meant to look if they were to be perceived as beautiful, it only messes up your self-esteem and worth. It's really an unhealthy way to inflict unnecessary torture upon yourself because what you see in magazines, social media, commercials, and so forth is simply not always what's real!

Thankfully, there are natural and healthy ways you can enhance and embrace your beauty all the more so that you not only enjoy being a great person on the inside but also a well-rounded beautiful person inside out. Let's now dive into the various ways you can develop a healthier relationship with your physical appearance.

How to Improve Your Body Language and Physical Health

Your body language entails how you carry yourself and what you communicate to others. Through your body language, you announce to the world who you are and what you believe in. Your demeanor basically tells a story about you. Taking ample time to develop your body language will help you to exude more confidence and also improve how you feel about yourself. There are certain body language characteristics that enhance your beauty and attractiveness. On the other hand, certain ways of carrying yourself can also lower your attractiveness and block your energy from shining radiantly. Let's unpack the various ways you can improve your body language so that your confidence can start shining brighter.

- **Posture:** Your posture entails the symmetry you have when you sit, walk, stand, or lay down. Poor posture can cause health issues such as back pain and neck pain, and reinforce a hunched back. Great posture is being able to maintain an upright position when standing or sitting. Slouching and having your head lean forward or backward when walking are all examples of asymmetrical postures that aren't good for your body. To develop a better posture, consider doing things like sitting or standing upright to avoid having a hunched back, stretching your muscles to help release tension, and taking up more space. When you slouch instead of walking with broad shoulders, it indicates a lack of confidence and makes you appear less attractive. Flexibility exercises such as tai chi and yoga are great examples of ways you can correct your posture and maintain a fit body.

- **Communication:** When you communicate, always strive for quality rather than quantity. This means that instead of rushing to say many things, focus on ensuring that your voice projection is high enough, your pace is slow and steady, and your gestures are also complementing what you are saying. When you speak it causes your body to feel more nervous and this can lead to increased fidgeting and signs of anxiety. Practice active listening by nodding your head when others are in communication with you; this enhances your attractiveness and makes you appear well-engaged.

- **Eye contact:** People can read our state through the eye contact we give. Practice maintaining good eye contact. When your eyes pace and wander around the ceiling or other places other than being directed to who you are speaking to, it makes you appear disinterested or rather aloof.

- **Diet:** How we look is massively impacted by the food we eat. A healthy diet packed with fruits, vegetables, and nutritious meals enhances your physical appearance and helps you have glowing skin. Taking multivitamin supplements is also recommended if you want to ensure that you do not miss out on all the nutrients your body needs. If you want to build muscle, taking a diet rich in protein helps. Things like eggs, lentils, legumes, fish rich in omega-3 fatty acids, and lean meat help to build a strong body. It's always best to avoid foods high in cholesterol and sugars, as these lead to obesity and can negatively affect your body.

- **Exercise:** While eating a great diet helps to grow the body you want, exercising helps you to get the shape you want. It's always a great practice to have at least ten minutes of your day devoted to exercise of any kind. If you want to improve your posture, exercises like cardio, planks, and ab workout routines help to tone the body well. Exercise does not always have to be rigorous; you can choose any rhythmic activity you enjoy such as dancing, and this too, if done consistently enough, helps to keep your body toned. Exercising also releases feel-good hormones such as dopamine and these in turn boost your confidence.

- There are several other body language turn-offs to avoid in order to improve your charisma. Things like pointing at others with your fingers, shouting, yelling, crossing your hands, not respecting people's personal space, and chewing gum while someone is talking to you can be perceived negatively.

Ways to Upgrade Your Personal Style

An undeniable way to develop massive confidence by enhancing your natural outward beauty is through upgrading your personal style. Your style is how you express who you are and what you stand for. When you develop a unique and strong sense of style, it sets you apart and makes you super attractive. People are drawn to people who love themselves, so what matters is that whatever style you choose for yourself, make sure it's something you will love and keep improving with time. Here are a few tips on how you can develop a great personal style:

- **Choose clothing that best compliments your body type:** What often lowers people's confidence is when they don't look good in what they are wearing. The blame is usually shifted, believing that perhaps you just don't have the superb body type. However, this couldn't be any further from the truth. Every body type has a specific clothing line that best compliments it. Your task is to simply discover what kind of clothes complement your looks and enhance your beauty.

- **Invest in a great skincare routine:** Our skin gets more complicated as we age. During adolescence, there are increased hormonal activities that cause things like acne, blackheads, and more skin issues. These won't simply go away with regular washes. Taking time to choose the right soap, toner, wash, scrub, and any other necessary products to solve the breakouts can help. Even as you age, your skin still faces a lot more problems. Hence, visiting a dermatologist and choosing the best skincare routine for yourself helps to keep your skin glowing, which in turn boosts your confidence. Using sunscreen helps to protect your skin from sun damage. Drinking adequate water should also be considered a pivotal part of your skincare routine, preferably nothing less than eight cups a day.

- **Style and grooming:** How we groom ourselves entails how tidy we keep our physical appearance.

Personal grooming entails things like making sure that your teeth are cleaned regularly, you smell good, your hair is always neat and well combed, and your environment is also maintained well. All these factors help you to enhance your beauty even more.

- **Sleeping well:** Without adequate rest, our bodies start to deteriorate and visible signs of fatigue can appear, such as having eye bags and general chronic pain. Choosing a specific time for going to bed and sticking to that routine helps to create healthy sleeping habits. Your body becomes accustomed to that routine and it gives it enough time for renewal and rest. Avoid eating late or being onscreen in the dark to protect your body and eyes from strain.

Now that we have explored ways you can enhance your physical beauty, let's find out how you have unstoppable confidence even in times when you don't feel great about yourself. Our confidence should not solely heavily rely on our looks and any other fleeting things. Those things are just meant to be complementary things. However, true confidence is rooted in what you believe about yourself and how you skillfully handle your challenges, limitations, and shortcomings.

CHAPTER 5

Thrive With Unstoppable Confidence

I truly believe in positive synergy, that your positive mind gives you a more hopeful outlook and belief that you can do something great means you will do something great. -
Russell Wilson

Unstoppable confidence is attainable through taking diligent actions in the right direction. Having a holistic approach to maintaining great confidence helps to ensure that every aspect of your life keeps thriving. Heavy reliance on just one thing to maintain your confidence keeps you at risk of losing your confidence completely when that one thing goes bad. For example, let's say you mainly feel confident about yourself because of your beautiful and stunning physical attributes; once those qualities start to experience challenges, your confidence crushes. Say one morning you wake up and notice that your face has had a massive breakout; would you still feel confident and have healthy self-esteem? Unfortunately for most people, their confidence is based on external factors, which makes it very easy for their confidence to get toppled over if their looks change.

Another problem is when people heavily rely on achievements to have confidence. There is nothing wrong with being confident because you are competent at work or in your social life. The only problem is that all those things are bound to change. It's not every day that you will always be successful in your pursuits and achieve recognition. In that case, your confidence would hit rock bottom whenever things don't go your way and escalate whenever things go well. This inconsistency in your confidence makes it hard to have healthy self-esteem because that kind of confidence is merely surface-level. There comes a point in your life when you have to finally feel free to embrace and fully accept who you are. This means that whether you are failing or winning, your head should always be kept high. Whether you are wearing makeup or not, you should still be able to fully feel confident in yourself. It is this unlimited confidence which is powerful and super attractive.

We all sometimes get addicted to a pattern of only feeling good about ourselves when we think things are going perfectly. Then when life knocks us down, we can fall into an unhealthy pattern of self-loathing, self-sabotage, self-doubt, and poor self-esteem. In a world where there are people who can prey on your weaknesses, allowing them to see this side of you can make it easy for them to consistently bring you down. However, if you choose to be someone grounded and unshakeable, always optimistic and positive when things are going well or not, this makes you incredibly powerful. To achieve this there are various mindsets you can learn to adopt. It is when we live our lives in that positive way that we start to attract so much abundance and draw closer to attaining our goals and dreams. We also start to inspire others around us to be more accepting and compassionate with ourselves because most people generally tend to reject themselves when they don't meet their expectations. This space you create for self-harmony makes you someone positive and pleasant to be around. When we judge and think low of ourselves when we perform below our expectations, it only erodes our confidence and that is why it is fundamental to learn ways to improve our perspective and overall outlook on things. Now let's unpack some of the obstacles that hinder people from having unstoppable confidence.

Overcoming Obstacles That Hinder Unstoppable Confidence

Obstacles that hinder unstoppable confidence comprise the internal and external limitations we may face. Internal limitations have to do with the weaknesses you have and external limitations have to do with things from your outside environment that threaten and impede your confidence levels. Below are examples of what those obstacles may be:

- **Perfectionism:** When we are consumed with wanting everything to go a certain way, our confidence can be crushed the moment things go another way. Thus, to ensure that your confidence is not negatively affected, leave room for unexpected outcomes. There are simply things that won't be in your control. Accepting that fact and focusing on what you can control and manage well will help you to maintain confidence. Introspect your standards of perfection and check if they might be what's stopping you from appreciating the beauty and value you already possess.

- **Fear and doubt:** Everyone has something they are afraid of and that's just a normal part of life. Your confidence should not only prevail when you don't feel afraid. This is why courage exists. It is the ability to take a certain course of action amid any sort of fear you might have. Confidence is learning to be at peace with knowing that despite how afraid you might be, you will still move forward and stand up for what you believe in. Doubt is when you second-guess yourself and that hesitancy wipes off any hint of confidence you might have had. The antidote to doubt is to simply have faith in yourself and embrace challenges with a positive frame of mind.

- **Indecision:** Confident people are extremely self-assured; they make clear and straightforward decisions. The more you avoid indecision, the more your confidence will grow much stronger. Take time to gain clarity on what your values are and the goals you wish to achieve. Knowing this ahead of time helps you to sift through what's right for you and what's not much easier when situations arise that require you to make decisions. Being able to stand by your decisions despite facing opposition or backlash from people reinforces your confidence and ultimately makes you gain the trust and respect of those who doubted you.

- **Negative self-talk:** To be a confident person, you have to be ferocious about silencing any form of negative self-talk. We all have an inner monologue that goes on every single day of our lives. That voice can either make or break you depending on whether you choose to believe what it says or not. We tend to be unkinder to ourselves than any other person can be. This is why we have to train our minds to generate more positive messages that empower instead of break us. To do this, you can start countering the negative messages by repeating daily affirmations that reinforce the beliefs you wish to live by. Finding your true purpose and identity also helps to protect you from any limiting narratives about who you supposedly are. Take time each day to cleanse your mind just as much as you prioritize cleansing your body. Wash away all forms of wrong ideologies and unreasonable expectations you or society may have imposed on you.

- **People pleasing:** When we try to live our lives constantly people pleasing, it gets exhausting and discouraging because it's hard to fully meet the demands of insatiable human beings with constantly changing expectations. This might make you feel like you aren't good enough or like you are worthless. Using people's expectations as a benchmark for measuring your value is an unfair way to treat yourself. Establish values of what matters to

73

you and have a priority list. Make that your focus instead of running after pleasing people who can change or be ungrateful. Find validation within yourself instead of scraping for it from others. This gives people an unfair advantage over you which they can use to break your confidence and lower your self-esteem. Become firmly grounded in what you think about yourself instead of relying on people's opinions to decipher your worth and significance.

- **Not asserting your boundaries:** Confident people are great at commuting their boundaries and maintaining them. If you notice that you lack boundaries or struggle to reinforce those you have, this might be what's stopping you from achieving unstoppable confidence. Boundaries protect you and what matters. Without them, people can walk over you and waste your time. Start practicing saying no confidently whenever you do not agree with something. Instead of just going with the flow, become someone who establishes what matters to you and self-advocates for it. The more we take our lives seriously, the more other people start to do the same too. Therefore, help people know the parameters in which they ought to operate with you and this will protect you from unnecessary problems.

- **Self-love deficiency:** When we lack self-love, it's hard to walk with your head held high unless you are just faking it. Self-love gives birth to self-acceptance and compassion. It liberates you and makes it possible for you to express yourself freely without the fear of judgment from others. Other people's opinions and negative influence only have a negative impact on you when you lose touch with your true self and lack self-love. To start loving yourself better, treat yourself like you would someone you deeply love and adore. The more you cultivate this sort of relationship with yourself, the more confident and appealing you will be.

- **Unhealthy expectations:** Have you ever met people who are so accomplished in many things yet still struggle with low self-esteem or poor confidence? It all comes from having unreasonable expectations of themselves. Since they only notice what they haven't achieved yet, they hardly see how much they already have going right for them. Learn to cultivate gratitude in your life and step-by-step, take time to move toward the higher goals you have without undermining where you already are. When you notice that you aren't where you want to be yet, simply seek advice and put in the work needed without putting yourself down.

Invest in Building Strong and Worthwhile Interpersonal Relationships With Others

The answer to being able to build and maintain positive relationships with others is learning to first build a great relationship with yourself. When you have a healthy and loving relationship with yourself, it sets the tone for how you will manage and build other relationships you will have. It's impossible to fully love and respect others when you don't love and respect yourself. Usually, when people try to love others at the expense of loving themselves, those relationships seldom ever work. Not loving yourself makes it come across to others as if you are indirectly saying there is something wrong with you that should make them question their decision to love you. This is why taking time to deal with any childhood trauma you might have had that makes it hard for you to love and accept yourself is pivotal to establishing healthy relationships for the rest of your life.

Loving yourself boosts your confidence in ways that other people's love for you can never do. There are many habits you can start adopting to build a life that promotes self-love and growth. These entail making your needs a priority and being your greatest friend and cheerleader. Instead of being the person who gets to reinforce all negative things about yourself, become your greatest encourager. Find ways to elevate your quality of life and upgrade your skills. The more you work on personal development, the more you will keep falling deeper in love with yourself. Find out what truly makes you happy and be willing to embrace that and fight for your dreams no matter what sort of opposition you face. When you make treating yourself well a habit, it becomes easy for you to naturally replicate that behavior in your relationships.

Usually, people who are mean to themselves tend to be mean to others and project their insecurities and anger on others. This is why relationships are really helpful in helping us to understand how much we love ourselves and know where to improve.

You can strengthen your relationship by having a growth mindset approach. Instead of ruling yourself out as someone who can't build relationships, challenge yourself to try. Saying you can't do something can just indicate laziness to learn. Therefore, embrace the challenge of regularly living outside your comfort zone and learning as many skills as you can. Relationships require us to have people skills and emotional intelligence. You have to have the ability to see through what others are saying and understand how they truly feel. People skills can be learned through working with a relationship coach, observing others, and reading books. If you isolate yourself, you lose the chance to make mistakes which can help you to learn and mature. Therefore, don't wait for you to be "perfect" before you start cultivating relationships. Know that where you are, you are worthy of companionship, and true relationships are those which allow you the room to grow.

You can develop beautiful relationships through communicating effectively, being accountable for your actions, being reliable, respectfully addressing conflicts directly instead of being passive-aggressive, allowing others to love and support you and also doing the same for them, having quality time, and being authentic in your interactions. Just like plants and flowers which thrive when they are watered and looked after well, relationships also flourish when we look after them well. These same relationships become an anchor to you and this fosters greater confidence and helps your self-esteem to improve too.

Dare to live a life filled with positivity and growth. It takes courage to not be ordinary and average. It takes wisdom to engage meaningfully with others and yourself. Create a lifestyle that is filled with so much positivity that it becomes hard for anything negative to take root. Escape any form of negative self-talk by facing your fears head-on and doing what you love. The more you create for yourself a beautiful life filled with so much gratitude and peace, the more you will attract great relationships. Your confidence flourishes when you know that you have a life of substance. Now let's dive even deeper into understanding how you can build massive confidence in your career—the kind of confidence which will enable you to keep experiencing career advancement.

CHAPTER 6

How to Be Confident in Social Situations

The way we communicate with others and with ourselves, ultimately determines the quality of our lives. -Tony Robbins

Being able to show up in a competent way socially is one of the keys to success. Our world revolves around people. Knowing how to deal with people effectively and present yourself in the best possible way can work to your best advantage. People are drawn to someone who shows signs of ease and social confidence. On the other hand, when you navigate your social life as if you are walking on eggshells, this only makes you emit a very anxious energy that can repel others from you once they sense it. Being confident in social situations is not just reserved for people who are more extroverted. It is a skill you have to develop regardless of your personality type. Sometimes, some people hide under the excuse that they are introverts and thus don't want to be around other people. The truth is that every human being has an inherent need for connection. Of course, our preferences may certainly vary when it comes to how much time we prefer being around others. Nevertheless, the point still stands that we all crave great social connections. Now the billion-dollar question is, how can you develop powerful social skills no matter the limitations you might feel you have? This chapter will unpack different strategies that you can employ and also help you to understand the root cause of social fears.

Your family, friends, neighbors, workmates, and the people you usually engage with all comprise your social environment. Sometimes you can feel very dissatisfied and rather disappointed with the quality of your social life because what you experience may not match what you expected. This disappointment has led many people to devise various strategies to overcome their social discontent, including moving to different geographical locations in the hope that they won't experience the same issues in another place. Ironically, life hardly ever allows anyone to thrive if they avoid facing the real problem. Moving to different locations might certainly make you experience a different culture, sometimes which is better than what you were exposed to previously. However, as I have grown to witness this multiple times—who we choose to be eventually shapes the quality of experiences we have in the long run. To elaborate on this point, consider this example: If you relocated to a different school because you wanted to escape being bullied, you may experience some peace temporarily. However, sooner than you would have imagined, you would start to see that pattern of being bullied starting to recycle itself again in your life. The seemingly easy way to solve this predicament would be to move to a different location again. However, this would never be a sustainable solution because no matter where you go, the law of attraction would always make you attract who you are. The same bullying would start to happen again. That is why learning how to face your social fears and also heal the wounds you have that were inflicted by your social experiences is the solution to short-circuiting that vicious cycle of being bullied.

This is exactly what happens with not just bullying but also many other social problems. If you struggle with making friends, being assertive, maintaining healthy boundaries, and being a free and confident person, the answer is not to look for solutions externally. The answer is to look into yourself and understand what it is about you that keeps making you attract that reality. Taking time to work on yourself and develop powerful social skills step-by-step ultimately enables you to attain the social freedom and joy that you long for.

When you look at people who are confident, sometimes we might feel discouraged thinking that they were just naturally born like that and assume that if we were to try to pursue confidence it would be a futile journey. The reality is actually that confidence is largely a result of your environmental conditioning. People who grew up with secure attachment styles and receive love and attention in a healthy way tend to grow up to be confident individuals and navigate their social relationships with more ease and enjoyment. Conversely, people who grew up with insecure attachment styles like being avoidant, anxious, disorganized, and fearful tend to have a harder time developing a healthy social life.

Thankfully, regardless of what sort of trauma you experienced growing up, you can still reprogram your mind and create healthy thinking patterns that will enable you to have a thriving social life. Now let's unpack some of the ways you can overcome anything that may hinder you from soaring socially.

Strategies for Overcoming the Fear of Rejection

The fear of rejection comes from the limiting beliefs people have about themselves. When you believe that you aren't worthy of thriving relationships and that you are too flawed to attract love and acceptance, you start to be afraid of social interactions because you won't want to see those fears become a reality. Coping mechanisms such as retreating from others, stonewalling, passive aggression, people pleasing, and playing small becomes the norm. Instead of being free to show your true self and confidently navigate through life with self-acceptance and respect, you start to exude so many insecurities and even live most of your life putting up a facade. This way of living with a mask on is exhausting and breaches your confidence because you would be well aware that you aren't being authentic. That awareness erodes your confidence because you would be feeling like a phony or as if you are living a fake life. Building relationships becomes extra difficult because people start to connect with the fake persona you are used to portraying. When they do connect to that fake persona, you start to feel like all your relationships are shallow and dissatisfying, which is understandable because you can only stop feeling alone if people connect with your true self.

The only way to put an end to that despondent lifestyle of trying to shape yourself into whoever you think people want you to be is to start practicing accepting and loving your true self. Think about it, wouldn't it be better to be accepted and loved by a few people and rejected by many because you are being your true self than being loved by many people for being the fake you? True confidence only shines when we are true to who we really are. What's most important is that as you start to embrace your true self and break free from the need to be validated by others at the expense of your validation, you start to truly love yourself more.

It's hard to love, respect, and be confident in a fake version of yourself. Once you peel off that mask and start showing up as your true self, it's like you just suddenly begin to have this foundation of love overflowing in your life that never runs dry. Suddenly you would start to feel alive and in touch with your true self. This makes you emit powerful magnetic energy because many people take a long time to reach those heights. A lot of people live their lives imprisoned by the fear of rejection and hence they too struggle with people-pleasing tendencies and living with a facade on. Being around someone who is authentic makes them feel hopeful and encouraged that it's possible for them too to break free from their limitations and fears. Generally, people like people who are like who they want to be. That means by being someone who is true to yourself, you naturally begin to attract many people because you would be someone they aspire to be someday. Stepping into the authentic version of yourself makes you shift your energetic dynamic to your favor and this makes your confidence soar beyond what anything you achieve externally can ever do to boost your confidence.

Building your confidence from this foundation allows you to have massive confidence that can withstand the test of time because it's grounded on the real version of who you are. The confidence that normally comes across as fake and only lasts briefly is confidence forged through acting like someone you aren't while denying your true values and needs. Even your heart would testify to you that you aren't being yourself. It's stressful to keep wearing a mask every day. Even when people do start to find you confident or like you, it's not the kind of validation that can satisfy your heart because it's based on the wrong foundation. Here are some of the ways you can start building authentic confidence and prepare yourself to be someone who can be socially competent:

- **Thoroughly deal with your past wounds and reparent yourself:** We all have in one way or the other been scarred by our past experiences. The wounds we incurred could have traumatized us so much that we would no longer want to attempt doing again what led us to have those experiences. The fear of reliving our pasts should never be avoided by choosing to play small and retreating to our shells like how a snail retreats from its shell when it feels threatened. For snails, doing that provides them with somewhat temporary protection, but it doesn't guarantee that the snail will be safe just because it chooses to hide in its shell. Any predator can still choose to step on the shell and harm the snail at any time. Also, being in the shell prevents the snail from moving forward. It can only move forward when it gets out there and exposes itself to the outside world. The same applies to our lives. Our past can make us feel afraid of taking risks and living outside our comfort zones. However, remaining in our comfort zones does not guarantee any safety and security at all; calamity can still strike us at any point in that seemingly same place. Our lives also stop progressing when we are hiding in our comfort zones. It's only when we step outside and embrace the opportunities life presents us that we would be able to thrive consistently. Will they be possible dangers when you put yourself out there socially? Yes! But will you still keep growing and learning new things? Yes! That means that, by choosing to shun relationships, you only stifle yourself and get in the way of your productivity and possible groundbreaking success.

- Reparenting yourself and correcting all false and negative beliefs you were accustomed to about yourself when you were younger will help you to start developing a secure attachment style. This means that in your social relationships, you will be able to start communicating your needs effectively and being secure. Instead of believing that people will reject you if you don't please them and deny yourself, you start being okay with accepting the fact that when someone rejects you it's okay. It's not a reflection of your inadequacies and you won't take things personally. You will give people the freedom to willfully choose you instead of being manipulative or possessive in your relationships just so you can avoid being left. People with a secure attachment style have healthy relationship habits such as also listening well to others and learning to be mutually supportive. You stop making it the responsibility of other people to keep you happy because you start to be confident in your ability to generate happiness for yourself. When others do offer to show you some love and meet your needs, it's done within healthy parameters instead of in toxic ways. Remind yourself that you are no longer a little child who is helpless and in danger. Now you are an adult who has the ability to protect yourself and provide for your needs. If others are invited into your life, it's an honor and they ought to treat it as such. Never settle for any kind of mistreatment socially. We teach people how to relate to us through the self-love we convey. Love yourself hard and watch your wounds heal fast and your life be completely transformed with more fulfilling connections.

- **Write a different blueprint and story for your life:** Unearthing the past wounds that lead you to be afraid of putting yourself out there socially also requires you to start rewriting a different script. Up until now, you have been living according to some beliefs that have been governing how you think about yourself and what you perceive about others. Those beliefs can be limiting and that is why you have to rewrite the beliefs that will start running your life moving forward. Take some ample time to draft a blueprint of the kind of life you wish to create for yourself. Have a clear mental image of what the confident version of yourself would talk, act, and think like, especially in social situations. Visualize and replay in your head how successfully your social interactions will go. This will raise the probability of what you imagined coming true in reality. Most of the things people end up doing in real life are first premeditated. And then once the opportunity strikes, people just start acting out a script that's already written. You too can do this for yourself!

- Become very clear about how you want your life to unfold. Chances are your subconscious mind will become very used to that script that when the chance comes for you to replay it, a neurological network for acting in line with what you envisioned would already have been formed in the brain. This makes it much easier and more automatic for you to act in ways that you long to. Cut ties with imagining the worst possible outcomes unfolding socially for you and start only maintaining positive thoughts about your present and future. Creating a different perspective and choosing to see everything that happens to you in a positive light helps you to confidently navigate through any social situation.

- **Regulate your emotions more effectively:** When we are emotional, we tend to see things in exaggerated or irrational ways. This is why the need to master emotional regulation is fundamental in connecting with others well socially. If people know you to be someone unpredictable and prone to outbursts of rage or mood swings, they start to avoid you because no one wants to be dealing with so much drama in their lives. Therefore, when you master emotional regulation, you begin to come across as someone well put-together and worthy of respect. Social interactions are more pleasant when people act harmoniously and handle conflict in healthy ways. Become familiar with peaceful dispute settlement instead of always throwing a fight every time you want to be heard and seen. People who are self-controlled gain more social leverage and are perceived to be more reliable and worthy of respect.

- **Practice empathy and compassion:** It's hard to connect with others when we hardly put in the effort to listen intently and understand where they are coming from. Empathy is being able to understand people and their different ways of reasoning. Without it, people lack societal acceptance and this can even lead to mental health challenges such as anxiety, depression, and panic attacks. Having empathy doesn't mean that you start acknowledging wrong things people do or say; it simply means being able to see the different ways people experience reality and allowing them the freedom and space to choose what's best for them. When we shove our ways and standards into people's faces and force them to live and reason the way we do, this only leads to conflicts and friction. Being socially competent entails learning different ways to communicate so that you can influence others to willingly commit to a worthwhile course of action.

- **Ditch neediness:** Many people who are needy simply emit energy that makes others find them repulsive. Neediness is not an attractive quality. It sends out a message that you are depending on others to meet your needs and this can cause people to feel pressured as they may not be in a position to meet your needs. The cure to neediness is to learn to love yourself and focus on self-validation instead of external validation. Neediness breeds a personality trait called codependency. This is when you have an unhealthy dependency on others for being happy or meeting your needs. It makes you treat others in unfair ways when they don't meet your expectations.

- **Reach out to others:** The only way to actually shine your light and make it known to others is to improve your social visibility. We can only be of great service to others when we make ourselves available for service. In our hiding place, no one will be able to connect with us. What would only be left are regrets of what could have been. Therefore, before it's too late, start taking the small strides necessary for building meaningful connections. Attending networking events and setting aside time for cultivating better social relations is how we can establish meaningful connections. When invited by friends or family to any social gatherings, instead of coming up with myriad excuses of why you can't go, dare to challenge yourself instead and just go. Yes, there is a level of uncertainty about how things will go since it will be new experiences. However, if we only commit our time to what we have certainty of and know, wouldn't our lives only be confined to those limited experiences alone? Punch any negative message that surfaces in your mind and always remind yourself that no matter what happens, what could honestly be the worst that can happen? You will be okay and your confidence is bound to thrive the more you put yourself out there.

- **Present yourself with class:** In the previous chapter, we looked into how you can make your personal style flourish. Your social life is what is most likely bound to flourish as you embrace an exquisite personal style and also present yourself with class. Having basic manners, communicating with the right tone, making sound decisions, and carrying yourself with class helps to heighten your ranking socially. People can only respond to what they see. So when they see someone with class, they will also start to be inclined to treat you with class instead of behaving in toxic ways around you.

How to Improve Your Communication Skills

Ultimately, the success of our social lives and building unstoppable confidence in our interactions is determined by your communication style. When you open your mouth, you immediately start teaching the people in your world who you really are and your world is highly likely to respond accordingly.

One of the most common mistakes people make when socially connecting is being unaware of the emotional state of someone and the non-verbal cues they are giving. For instance, if someone looks worried, and seems to be in a rush, that is not the right time to bring up a sensitive lengthy topic that will need their full attention and prolonged time. If they start to act disinterested in what you are saying, it might affect your confidence and make you second-guess whether you didn't earn their respect. It can also make you have all sorts of conclusions about why that interaction didn't go well, which is why it's important to first assess the situation before engaging in any conversation.

When facing volatile situations, it's important to be okay with being a mature person and advocating for peace and harmony. Sometimes most social connections fail because no one is confident enough to address the elephant in the room and say they are sorry. Being able to communicate how remorseful you are about anything that may have gone wrong helps people to trust you more and be willing to work toward improving things. Every time something goes wrong, there are always two sides to the story. Having social wisdom is giving people on both sides the opportunity to explain their story and then decipher a fair way forward without coming across like you are taking sides.

There are many things you can pick up when you observe people's body language. This is why active listening is important for having great conversations. Learning to be concise and straight to the point in your communication also helps to prevent misunderstandings or people zoning out on you while you are speaking. Now let's unpack the ways you can start building massive confidence in your career life.

CHAPTER 7

How to Build Confidence in Your Career

I always did something that I was a little not ready to do. I think that's how you grow. When there's that moment of, Wow, I'm not so sure that I can do this; and you push through those moments, that's when you have a breakthrough. Sometimes that's a sign that something really good is about to happen. You're about to grow and learn a lot about yourself. -Marissa Mayer

Your career is your source of getting income to meet your survival needs and a place of self-expression. It takes up a huge chunk of your life most days. Learning how to bring out the best in yourself in that environment leads to a more fulfilling life. Without peace and career advancement, it's hard to live a happy life. Understanding the things that impede your success in this area can help you to overcome those limitations and grow your strengths and achievements.

Confidence is one of the biggest and most powerful assets anyone can ever have in their career field. It is the confident people who inspire others to have faith in them. It is the self-assured individuals who boldly take on challenges and keep progressing in their careers. On the other hand, people who are lacking in confidence, are reluctant, timid, unsure of themselves, and constantly bombarded by the imposter syndrome play small and hardly achieve their full potential.

Before others can have faith in you and be comfortable with trusting you with responsibilities, they first need assurance from you that you believe in yourself and you will show up when needed. There won't always be people who are kind enough to just entrust more responsibilities to you despite seeing your obvious lack of confidence in yourself. Only moving forward when you are pushed by those kind-hearted co-workers or superiors limits and delays your achievements. This is why it is of absolute importance to cultivate career competence and confidence on your own.

One of the main obstacles that block many high achievers from fully attaining their potential is the feeling of imposter syndrome. This is when you feel like no matter how much you have accomplished so far, those achievements were merely luck and you didn't deserve them. This feeling and belief is so paralyzing because it can stop you from fully realizing your true potential. You chronically walk around feeling like a phony and afraid that others will someday realize that you were inadequate after all.

Many people have shied away from taking on new responsibilities or accepting promotions and opportunities that could have taken them to higher dimensions of their careers because of feeling and believing that they are inadequate. This toxic perspective comes from long-term limiting beliefs that might have taken root in your subconscious. For instance, if you grew up in an environment where people constantly put you down and laughed at you if you spoke about your dreams and goals, this might make you second-guess yourself. The result of this dynamic is that no matter what you achieve, you start struggling to own those successes and enjoy them because of feeling like you stole them away from someone or that it's not your place to achieve so much.

The imposter syndrome makes people start isolating themselves as they feel safer in a place of hiding rather than being in high-exposure job positions, which makes them feel vulnerable to criticism and being discovered as a fraud. We also see it when people start to overthink so much when it's their turn to give input and contribute. They may be filled with thoughts like *Why would people want to listen to me? I haven't even aligned with all the principles of what I am about to teach, it's hypocritical of me to even have a say in this matter. My teammates are better than me, I will let them take that role and avoid advocating for myself. I deserve to be punished for every mistake I make; other people's mistakes aren't so bad. I can never get that promotion; others are just way more competent and talented than me.* This sea of negative messages swirling in your mind can make you miss out on many opportunities or career advancement. Your fears also start to replicate in reality the more you notice that others keep getting ahead and you are left behind.

Thankfully, there is a way to reverse that crippling mindset and build a more positive frame of mind through cognitive restructuring. This is when you start neutralizing all those limiting beliefs by reinforcing more powerful beliefs through positive affirmations such as saying things like

- I am a premium-level asset to my career; I bring forth the best results possible.

- I am so talented, gifted, and wise. Anyone would be lucky to have my work with them.

- There is nothing I can't do because that is why learning is there. With time and effort, I can acquire the necessary skills I need to carry out successfully any given task within reasonable parameters.

- I am not defined by the mistakes I made; instead, I am a constantly evolving individual capable of progressive success.

- I don't believe that others are better than me or less capable than me. I believe that we are all uniquely gifted with individual strengths that are beneficial to any collective purpose.

- I work very hard and deserve to enjoy and celebrate every part of my achievements.

It is important to note that just because you feel a certain way doesn't mean that your feelings are a true reflection of reality. When someone is caught up in a negative cycle of imagining the worst about themselves and others, they start to view life through distorted lenses. You may even start to feel like people are out there to get you and conspire against you when people are often just consumed with their own lives. It's easier to fall into the pattern of self-sabotaging in your career and this is why we have to unpack different ways you can cultivate a positive frame of mind and make better choices that can help your confidence to soar in the corporate world.

How to Navigate Workplace Dynamics and Self-Advocate

What are those carefree childhood beliefs and dreams you used to have about yourself? When people are young, they are usually free from many fears which they start to acquire over time as years go by. Remembering how you used to perceive the world and yourself will help you to notice the difference between the healthy way you used to decode reality and how far you may have strayed from that positive outlook on life. Write down the list of all the things you used to genuinely believe you are capable of achieving. Ask yourself, if it were not for your fears and false beliefs, what could your career have been like by now? Would you even be working in the field you are in now? If you were no longer held back by the imposter syndrome, what would you go after? These questions will help you to become enlightened about the possible life you should be living and stir up a powerful will to fight for your true life and be freed from the prison of living with imposter syndrome.

In a workplace environment, your attitude and work ethic matters a lot. Without putting in place boundaries and self-advocating, you can be taken advantage of by others or not noticed for your effort. This is why it's extremely important to decide how you will conduct yourself in a work environment so that your behavior invites the positive outcomes you desire. Below are different strategies you can put in place to avoid burnout and short-changing yourself:

- **Delegation:** One of the things people shy away from when they lack confidence is delegation. Delegation requires you to communicate with others and potentially face resistance. This dynamic is uncomfortable and makes many people end up overworking themselves instead of rightfully allocating different responsibilities to the people who have to carry them. Avoiding delegation can give you the illusion that people will like you because you didn't give them more work to do, but that is rarely ever the case. People seldom respect someone who can't stand up for themselves. So what it does is that it only makes you appear weak and like an easy person to manipulate. This is why despite feeling nervous or afraid, it's important to still put yourself out there and assertively make everyone accountable for the work they have to do. It's hard to get into a leadership position and succeed in it if you avoid delegation. Being a leader requires you to be good at motivating others to do their part. If you are the only person carrying the load because of fear to get everyone to work, things won't work out.

- There is only so much you can do with your strength. So practicing how to keep everyone accountable and following up on if things are done is fundamental for succeeding in the workplace. Your confidence can only grow if you practice various ways to communicate effectively. In time, you will start understanding what the effective ways to communicate are and what doesn't work. This will also help your confidence to elevate. To help you delegate effectively, practice assigning roles as early as possible; this helps you to get a better response from people when you do reach out. Also, the roles have to be clear, and double-checking if everyone understands helps to ensure that the work is done.

- **Self-advocacy:** Self-advocacy entails standing up for your values and rights. Let's say someone tried to take advantage of you because of their superior position; this is when you would have to advocate for yourself by stating what you will accept and what you won't accept. Self-advocacy helps people to understand your needs and know how to treat you. It ensures that offenses are not repeated. Making your skills known and taking credit for your work is also self-advocacy. Sometimes in the workplace people may try to take credit for what you did and this may result in you falling behind while they get ahead.

This is why it's important to be confident about your rights and stand up for them. Without confidence in the workplace, you can end up being used or overworked, and under-compensated for your efforts. Another dire and unjust thing that can happen in any work environment if people don't confidently advocate for themselves is being sidelined, bullied, and harassed. This can go on for a long time, ending up making the workplace environment a toxic place to be in. Ultimately, your mental health and career advancement can be affected when self-advocacy is lacking.

- **Know when to say "No":** One of the main struggles people face when they lack confidence in the workplace is overworking themselves. No matter how much they achieve, they would still undermine their accomplishments and set the bar so unreasonably high for themselves. This attitude makes it hard for people to appreciate you since you yourself won't be setting a good example of appreciating your efforts. It invites people to have unhealthy expectations of you. This is why learning to say "No" is pivotal to your well-being in the workplace. Being someone who says yes to almost anything and everything happens because most people tend to be insecure about themselves and thus try to gain approval from others by denying their needs and putting what other people want first. Being confident enough to say no makes other people have confidence in you as they get to see how true you are to yourself. Maintaining those workplace boundaries also helps you to avoid burnout and end up jeopardizing your health and peace due to a precarious workload and unending unhealthy expectations from others. Always set realistic and attainable expectations for yourself, bearing in mind that your career is just one aspect of your life. You still have your health, relationships, spiritual life, and mental well-being to look after. If all those aspects of your life are also looked after well then they too also start to be your joy and source of confidence and peace.

- **Upskill:** The most confident people in the workplace are those able to keep up with the demands of what's needed in a dynamic environment. Your skills may be needed for a certain duration, but if they aren't developed your competence level can end up being shallow than the rest of others. This affects your confidence because you would start to appear as someone with less experience. Upskilling helps you to grow your confidence in completing different roles. When you fail to gain a high position because of your skill level, instead of believing that you aren't good enough for that role, it's better to focus on developing yourself instead. Through learning new things, your abilities improve and your competence level grows. Sometimes workplaces provide opportunities for upskilling but only relying on those opportunities limits your growth. It's always wise to take the personal initiative to invest in your personal upskilling programs outside work. This could range from taking a paid course, enrolling in free courses available online, or having a mentor who can coach you to perform better than you have been. Upskilling is one of the best ways to also achieve our self-actualization needs. We all desire to see the higher and better versions of ourselves, and your career is certainly an area where you can achieve those goals.

- **Create a network of supportive co-workers:** A work environment can be unbearable without genuine friendships and good working relationships with others. Consider taking the first steps to indicate to others that you are keen on building a relationship with them. When you don't show interest in others, it's easy for them to assume that perhaps you don't deem them as good enough for your company or many other negative things. People are generally filled with the fear of rejection, so the slightest perceived sign that you may possibly be rejecting someone can be taken seriously. This is why being wise in your interpersonal relations entails also being able to reassure others through your words and actions that you wish them well and like or respect them. It's most likely that the kinder and more verbal you are about your good intentions for others, the more likely people will likely not see you as a threat. Take time to do meaningful things to build a strong support network of friends and co-workers who can support you when you need help. Being a source of support for others also helps you to create stronger relationships. Relationships provide a sense of belonging and security, which is a fundamental human need we all have. This is why creating a friendly and harmonious work atmosphere through having great connections with others is helpful for your career and overall well-being. Usually, people who don't have good relationships with others and are normally isolated tend to struggle with a lack of confidence.

- Even if you are an independent person who is confident, there is still a greater level of confidence you can attain by knowing that you have people supporting and rooting for your success. Building relationships is fairly easy, it's in the small and big things consistently done with a heart of sincerity that people start to develop a fondness for you. Examples of these heart-warming acts can be asking someone if they would like to join you for lunch, offering to help lift weights, supporting someone's idea in a discussion, standing up for someone when they are being mistreated, sharing positive words of affirmation, and so many other brilliant ideas I'm sure you can think of.

- **Treat everyone with respect:** Your career can be negatively affected by people's perception of you. Being mindful of the way you treat others can help to save you from many possible issues that may arise due to conflicts and misunderstandings. It's hard to always be confident in an environment where everyone is mad at you or assuming that you are out there to get them. This is why it's important to always make an effort to help people understand your goodwill toward them. The more you respect others, the more likely it is that they too will reciprocate that treatment to you. When being considered for promotions and possible collaborations, many factors are looked into—things like your competence, reliability, and also how you work well with others. If your reputation is pleasant and many people can attest to having meaningful and respectful engagements with you, it will certainly work to your advantage. However, if a panel of individuals was to be interviewed about the way you treat others, if you know that your track record with that isn't good, this would dwindle your confidence. It would be highly likely that they will leave a bad review about you, which will possibly adversely affect your career.

- **Consistency and reliability:** It's one thing to be able to perform well for a season but to maintain success for a long time is another thing. True reliability is seen through the test of time. True confidence comes from being truly reliable instead of acting reliable. In a work environment, it's easy for many people to appear as someone they are not and as they do so it may come across as if those people are very confident. However, all those masks wear off in due time since it's not easy to keep pretending to be who you aren't. There are many people who manage to get ahead in their careers through deceitful ways and pretentiousness. In the eyes of the people they manage to deceive, of course, that's not what they will be perceived as. It's like a skill many people have to make others believe what they want them to believe, which is often far from the truth. You might be tempted to also start acting in the same deceitful ways to get ahead like others who seem to be climbing up the ladder so far. However, a house built on an unreliable and false foundation soon shakes and falls apart once turbulent times come. So having the wisdom and discretion to understand that trying to get ahead using unfaithful means is rather a snare. Your confidence in your career can only be sustained if you manage to uphold noble values and advance through the proper channels and ways. The confidence gained from acting deceitful and temporarily seeming like you are winning only falls apart in the end.

- Thus, to have lasting confidence and peace of mind in your career, it's always important to avoid any kind of temptations of getting ahead through unjust ways. Group conformity is one of the greatest tests many people face in their careers. If you get in most work environments, they all have a certain culture they uphold. Sometimes that culture might be negative and other times it may be good. It's important to also ensure that your confidence is not based on being one with a culture that is toxic. This is because it dims your light and prevents you from helping others to be inspired to have confidence based on adhering to the correct and noble culture and norms. It only takes a few people who choose to stand for what is right for a whole multitude of other people to also join in advocating for having confidence that is based on doing what is just and right. When your career is founded on noble principles and ways, you won't have to live with the fear of being exposed to have been a fraud or schemer. Create a future with hope and certainty for your career by being someone of necessity and having a genuinely righteous work ethic.

- **Treat yourself like you are a star worker:** You are responsible for showing and announcing to the world that you are a person of great significance and ability. It's not wise to leave the power of making that known up to other people. You have to pioneer that journey of ensuring that who you are and the unique contributions you have to make to your career are made known. You make known to everyone that you are a diamond and star through how you treat yourself. It's seen through how you announce and uphold your boundaries. It's also seen through how you treat others. People who do not love and believe in themselves have a hard time knowing how to love and believe in others too. Rather, most of their behaviors are directed toward inflicting their hurt and projecting their insecurities onto others too. Become a person of great character by working on loving yourself better than ever before. The more you learn to love yourself dearly, the more likely you would be able to also start loving others better and uplifting those you work with. Treat yourself with high regard no matter what. That means whether you are performing excellently or struggling in your career, you still need to treat yourself with respect, love, and compassion. Continue to speak well of yourself and never downgrade your career goals just because of a season of difficulties. Once you master showing yourself unconditional love, that's also when the world around you starts to radiate that same kindness and treatment toward you. Your confidence should not only shine in seasons when your career is flourishing, but it should also remain intact and shining even during times of hardship and uncertainty.

- **Emit positive energy:** It's hard to always show up motivated at work. It's easier to be someone who complains and grumbles about all sorts of things seemingly not going well. However, it takes great discipline to cultivate a positive frame of mind and commit to only uttering things that elevate others. When you are known to be someone who confidently advocates for positivity when it would have been much easier to just join the crowd and be negative, this would be the true essence of a leadership spirit.

Every time you notice people downcast or things not going well, always remember that contrary to what many people would think that things will go downhill, adversity can turn into a tremendous blessing if you choose optimism. It's when it's dark that stars and lights become significant and serve their purpose. Likewise, even in your career path, never allow yourself to be intimidated by challenges because they are simply opportunities for explosive growth depending on your attitude and perspective. To consistently maintain positivity, you have to be able to rise above your emotions and feelings and master self-control and discipline. This means that even when you may not feel like being courteous to someone who hurt you at work, you still treat them with kindness and class. Even though you may not feel like completing your work the right way, you still do it cheerfully and faithfully.

- Emotional regulation is fundamental in ensuring that you do not lose momentum but can keep being positive despite what happens. When you become someone who stays in character despite being tempted to be negative and throws in the towel, this makes you very appealing to superiors looking for prospective leaders. Your confidence and positivity should always shine no matter what season it is. This also means that, in the background, you have to brainstorm and find ways to problem-solve. If your happiness and confidence in your career only surface when things go well, then it will become easy to be knocked down by life at any time. To prevent that roller coaster ride, always mindfully exercise patience, positivity, and self-discipline.

- **Celebrate your triumphs:** We all have goals and these goals can either bring us so much happiness or be the reason why we feel horrible about ourselves. High achievers have a tendency to undermine their small achievements and only focus on big goals they haven't yet achieved. While this may come across as a noble quality, it is actually very bad for your mental health and it can also demoralize those around you. Happiness should not only be limited to arriving at the destination or when you achieve all your goals. Your happiness should be experienced in every step of the way you take. Every progressive step forward deserves acknowledgment and celebration. When you become someone appreciative of your efforts it makes you such a pleasant person to be around and work with. It also inspires so much motivation and a positive atmosphere that encourages others to keep doing better. Imagine if you had an employer who never acknowledges or celebrates your efforts, wouldn't that be a discouraging environment to work in? If the answer is yes, why is it that sometimes we are okay with treating ourselves that way? Your confidence can only blossom when you cultivate a grateful heart and embrace the journey and all the efforts you make with a thankful spirit. The more you voice how thankful you are for how far you've come, that's also how others will take notice of what they may not have known about your hard work and this can positively impact your career. On the other hand, if you are constantly saying negative things about your career progress and efforts, you also influence people's perception of you to change according to the undermining way you view yourself. They too would start to feel that you aren't doing your best and this can lead to more pressure and unreasonable expectations being imposed on you. Appreciate your sweat, the mere fact that you manage to get out of bed each day and show up for work is cause for celebration.

Normalize Taking Positive Risks

One of the best ways to advance in your career is to be a positive risk-taker. Without taking calculated risks, you miss out on so many opportunities for growth and development. Once someone has a good career and they get a hang of it, the temptation to just settle and remain comfortable in their newfound source of security is always high. The fact that you would feel like your life is better than it used to be when you were jobless can be good but also negative at the same time. It becomes a negative thing if it makes you only compare your success with your past achievements. If you feel like where you are currently is the best place you could ever be because it's much better than your past achievements, you may fall into complacency and lose sight of many other opportunities available for you to grow and achieve greater heights in your career. This is why adopting a mindset of taking on risks positively can help you to achieve greater dimensions you may possibly have never thought possible.

Taking risks can feel utterly terrifying, especially if you are someone who overthinks. What helps to take risks that would have a high probability of success is consulting with other people more experienced. Getting advice and feedback from people who are more knowledgeable of the areas you wish to take risks in helps you to avoid making misinformed and unwise decisions. Many people who tend to thrive and be successful risk-takers in their careers have so much confidence in what they are doing because they know that they will already be standing on the shoulders of great giants who are proven to already have mastered that territory.

Your career should be a place that allows you to grow and discover multiple versions of yourself that represent a more developed view of you. Careers are not meant to be like prisons that keep you bound to one responsibility, the same low salary until your life ends. Careers are meant to provide the space for you to discover what truly makes you happy and what you excel in. Once you do know what it is that makes you happy and which you can perform as naturally as possible, this is when you have to recognize that everything has a time. Some jobs you take in your first few years are simply meant to help you to gain confidence, manage expenses, and discover the next step for you. Having a job doesn't mean that now you just have to settle for living the same way every day. People who are great at bringing out the best in themselves always seek to improve their skills and experience by embracing new challenges. Even the jobs you may have applied to before have a pivotal role to play in the success of your career. When your mind is just focused on getting the position, if you get declined it may feel like you wasted all your time applying for the job and putting in so much work for it for nothing. However, this is hardly ever the case for most people. There are so many lessons you can master from your rejected applications. Usually, people receive feedback on what made their application to be denied. If you don't receive feedback, it's always a good practice to ask so that you can become aware of what you need to work on in order to improve in the future.

As you work on yourself by taking into consideration the constructive feedback you would have been given, it makes you more experienced and knowledgeable than you were before. It increases the chances of you being a more competent and well-prepared future candidate for most jobs because failure often equips us all with so many lessons we may never have learned if we never tried taking risks. Trying to get a better profession is a positive risk in itself. This is because you risk losing so much in the application process and you also risk facing failure, which may make you feel bad about yourself. However, just making the effort to keep trying to attain better heights helps you to develop immunity against rejection. You start learning to not personalize things. Taking risks also helps you to create a better life for yourself. Every time we as humans don't do what we know is meant to help bring out the best in us, we feel bad and almost ashamed of ourselves. Now imagine what would happen if you normalize taking risks. Wouldn't that develop greater confidence in you and make you more courageous to set greater goals and chase them?

No matter how much success you may have acquired so far in your career, always remember that there are more places for you to go, more skills that will improve your skill level and expertise, and more opportunities to earn better and work in toxic-free environments. The moment you start feeling comfortable with your job, start taking that as a sign that it's time to wake up and keep moving forward. The more experienced you become in doing many different things, the more your confidence will blossom and just shine so brilliantly. What's been holding you back from creating the career experience you have always wanted to have? Challenge yourself and start reaching out to doors you may haven't knocked on before when comfort and complacency used to blind you from noticing that there is so much more to life than just your current career. You can grow, experience adventures, and most importantly, build relationships that are so fulfilling because of your grounded and irresistible confidence. In the last chapter we are about to dive in, we will now unpack the various ways you can maintain confidence and keep unleashing better versions of yourself.

CHAPTER 8

How to Maintain and Keep Growing Your Confidence

Life is not easy for any of us. But what of that? We must have perseverance and above all confidence in ourselves. We must believe that we are gifted for something and that this thing must be attained. -Marie Curie

What is your core belief about confidence? Do you perhaps believe that you can only be confident if you achieve so many things and without many accomplishments, you have no ground for being a confident person? Sadly, many people uphold this belief and it tremendously prevents them from being confident because once you achieve something, there is always something else you wouldn't have achieved yet that can make you feel insecure. Your life essentially becomes like a rat race where you are constantly on the run chasing after something you can never really attain with that ideology. The great news is that confidence is actually a trait you can create and it all starts from within. Lasting confidence should never be based on your external accomplishments, including the material possessions you have, because all those things are bound to fluctuate. One day you may have many things and perform well, and the next day may be a different story. It's impossible to be consistently confident and grounded if you are always looking outside yourself for confidence. Sometimes other people's confidence is based on the associations they have with people they consider to be in high regard. The danger of also basing confidence on the associations one has is that relationships also don't always last and when you aren't those people who make you feel confident, your confidence will keep sinking. It's such a wonderful thing to know that we don't have to have super achievements and be liked by many people before we can start to be confident. You can achieve massive confidence by tapping into your inner worth and creating confidence. Yes, *you can create confidence*!

Knowing that you can create confidence liberates you from being needy and depending on others to make you feel confident. It saves you from wasting time waiting for the so-called *perfect* version of you that is usually based on the wrong idea of what perfection entails. Many people believe that the perfect version of themselves is an accomplished individual who is succeeding in every area of their life and is always happy. This idea is a delusional understanding of what perfection entails because life always presents us with opportunities to grow beyond our current accomplishments. The question becomes, how can people create and maintain lasting confidence now?

Several factors can help you create lasting confidence and we will unpack them now.

- **Embody a state that exudes confidence:** Your state is essentially your mood and how you are. You can either be someone who chronically feels unhappy, demotivated, unsure of yourself, and afraid. Or you can be someone who chooses to generate feelings of positivity and maintain an optimistic outlook on life, be cheerful, hopeful, energetic, and motivated. Confidence has a lot to do with how you feel. Just as there are certain things that can make you feel happy or angry, there are also many things that can make you feel confident. Tapping into those things that allow you to feel confident will help you change your state. One of the most pivotal ways to change your state is to make your physiology match someone who is confident. For instance, many people who lack confidence can be seen avoiding eye contact, taking up very little space, slouching, talking very fast or with a too-low voice projection, handing their heads down, walking into a room, and focusing on their phones whenever they feel anxious, and so many other things. This body language makes you come across as very shy and not confident. Before you even start speaking verbally, that physiology would have already spoken volumes to those around you that you don't feel confident in yourself. On the other hand; if someone were to walk into a room with their head raised high, chin up, chest out, shoulders broadened, smiling, giving people firm handshakes, giving direct eye contact, taking nice and sturdy strides as they are walking, you would certainly know immediately that that's someone very confident. By simply embodying that body language, it positively affects how you feel and you start to emit very great energy. Even if you weren't feeling confident before, moving and carrying yourself in such a way will automatically make you feel and appear confident! All you have to do is to decide to show up how a confident person would.

- **Mindfulness meditation:** Sometimes our minds wander and become so fixated on the mistakes we made before and all the things that are possibly not going well. This can give you overwhelming emotions of feeling like you are a failure and it can impede your confidence. Hence, being mindful of where you focus becomes extremely crucial in maintaining confidence. What we focus on determines where our energy and resources will flow. This means if you are always ruminating on all the things you think are wrong about you, those things become more reinforced instead of fading away. For this reason, when creating healthy habits, people are always recommended to focus on the great habits they want to have instead of focusing on their bad habits. By focusing on your positive habits, you make the most of your energy and resources available for creating those habits in reality. As you create those great habits, they take up more of your space, making it impossible for the negative habits to still be there. Similarly, when you are building your confidence, there is no need to obsess about your weaknesses, mistakes, and limitations; doing that only impedes your energy from flowing where it should be. Instead, you can simply focus on how you want to be. The more you mindfully think about how the confident version of yourself would live your life, the more likely you are to replicate what you are envisioning in reality. Since our minds are always bombarded with thousands of different thoughts every day, it's best to train and rewire them so that they become more inclined to obsess over the confident version of ourselves, and by doing so we naturally start to fall into the ways of how a confident person would move about.

- Taking time each day, especially in the early mornings to deeply think about the kind of person you want to be that day helps you to create a mental blueprint of how you can carry yourself. That blueprint will then become your guide throughout the day, helping you to remember the beauty of the confident version of yourself. The probability of replicating that powerful image of yourself and the confident life you wish to manifest becomes extremely high whenever you meditate mindfully each day about it. This is because we naturally become attracted to what we think the most about. To embody lasting confidence, always remember to always control your thoughts and channel them toward forming pictures of what you want to see, not what you don't want to be anymore or what you did wrong.

- **Remember to always live in the present:** There is no doubt that many of the things that hinder people from being confident are the ancient stories they tell themselves about how inadequate they are and what they supposedly can't accomplish. It's those lies we feed ourselves about how we don't deserve this and that because of all sorts of invalid reasons. We make ourselves suffer so much because of not letting go of those unhealthy stories and limiting beliefs. Instead of realizing that today is a new day where you are able to create an amazing life for yourself, you may continue to be trapped in the past, viewing yourself as the old version of yourself and reliving your undesirable past experiences. Mindful meditation helps your mind to be centered in the present. Remember that you are not who you used to be, nor are you defined by your mistakes, opinions of others, and limiting beliefs. You have the power to decide who you want to be and you can embrace that version of yourself fully without having to feel like an imposter. The more you practice living in the present, the easier it will be for you to channel most of your energy toward creating the new you. Being stuck in the past drains your energy and makes you less aware of all the wonderful opportunities for building a great life available to you. Start to focus on creating an amazing life for yourself one day at a time. Don't worry or overly focus on too many things at the same time, just channel your energy toward being the confident version of yourself you can be today. As you manage to show up each day in empowering ways, this ultimately compounds to be weeks, months, and years of you being a confident and grounded person.

- **Leverage proximity:** Being around people who are confident and empowering is very important for maintaining your confidence. If you are constantly in the company of people who put you down and instill a negative mindset in you, it's very likely that their way of thinking will also end up affecting your confidence negatively. By increasing your proximity to people who mentally stimulate and encourage you to become more grounded in your confidence, you are likely to no longer slip into negative states that impede confidence. People living in our generation have the advantage of having extensive and easy access to so many resources that can help them grow and maintain their confidence. If you are someone who doesn't like reading hard-copy books, there is the option of listening to audiobooks and podcasts on building confidence. There are also many resources of ways to build confidence that you can tap into and study online to continue to grow your knowledge and understanding of how to improve your confidence. What is more effective in building confidence is pushing yourself to be in more real-life situations that require you to exercise confidence. Joining social clubs, going to watch sports with others, attending family gatherings, attending networking events, and visiting many other places where you can hone your skills. Having people who can help you with some feedback on ways to improve your confidence also provides you with other sets of eyes that can make you aware of what you may have missed.

Principles of a Confident Person

When pursuing confidence, it's important to have principles that will push you to always stay committed to a life of living confidently despite the need to sometimes give up or just become complacent about it. When people have principles, values, and core beliefs they decide to align their lives to, it protects them from allowing undesirable experiences from keeping on repeating themselves. It also helps them to create an environment that supports their confidence goals. Consider taking the time to think about the kind of principles you can commit to for you to always be a confident person. For instance, if someone wants to be a leader, they would need to have principles they uphold which would make them a great leader. Examples of these can be to set the principle that they would never go past a week without taking the time to engage with the people they are responsible for to know their condition and see how best they can serve them. If you have this principle as a leader, it makes you succeed so much in your leadership role because how can someone be a great leader if you don't regularly check on the well-being of the people you are leading? Similarly, to be a confident person, you too have to establish the principles you will operate in that will enable you to always have lasting confidence throughout your life. Let's have a look at some of the suggested principles you may have to support your confidence journey.

- **Believe in your unique abilities and always grab opportunities to harness them:** You have a unique contribution to bring to this world that no one else can ever replicate. You are born with skills, gifts, talents, and abilities that will help to make the world a better place, starting with your own sphere of influence. Discovering those qualities should be your greatest joy, but most importantly, putting them to use. You can know more about those strengths and gifts by receiving feedback from those who know you well. I'm sure as you navigate through life you always notice something very unique about the people around you. At times, most people are unaware of their strengths and tend to even take them lightly or just disregard them. Since it's something you may be naturally good at, you may fail to see how great of a significance that quality has and the impact it has in helping others. This is why taking time to work with a coach or personal mentor who can help you to delineate your strengths and find ways to improve and use them is important in helping you grow your confidence. Normally those strengths you have can also help you to have an idea of what your purpose and calling is.

- People who succeed so much in life don't necessarily do so because of being good at many things, but it's usually because they embrace what they are extremely good at and work hard to become a guru in that field. We see this with celebrities who become so popular and achieve massive financial breakthroughs because of just narrowing down their focus and honing their best talents. If you decide to no longer undermine your unique talents and abilities, this will open great doors for you to unlock a level of success that only you can achieve in that dimension because you were essentially designed for it. Sometimes our confidence is deflated simply because we focus on the wrong things. Therefore, find at least one to three things you are extremely naturally good at and start building your life around supporting those talents. This gives you a massive and unbeatable competitive advantage that will also boost your confidence greatly.

- **Establish a routine that empowers your confidence:** Life can get really messy when our lives are devoid of solid structures and routines that support maximum efficiency and growth. As we discussed earlier, starting your day with empowering exercises such as mindful meditation, taking a run while you visualize how you want your day to unfold, and doing any exercises that relieve you of stress and anxiety can help you sustainably maintain confidence. Think about it: During the days when you didn't have a clear goal and allowed yourself to sleep overtime, eat unhealthy food, and just randomly go about your days, would you say you felt confident? Chances are that it is highly unlikely that you felt confident because having messy days makes you feel like you do not have control over your life. You would start to feel like a failure and even the prospect of leading others would feel ridiculous because how can you help others create an efficient life if your life is a mess? Therefore, having a healthy routine should always be a non-negotiable practice for each day of your life. Whenever you are tempted to not establish and keep a healthy routine, always remind yourself that that act is a clear violation of your self-respect. It's hard to be confident when we don't respect our time. Avoid the unnecessary stress and turmoil that comes with being disorganized and lacking control over your life. When you intentionally respect each day of your life and treat it with utmost dignity, you become more confident because your life, and not just you, will be a living testimony of how efficient, reliable, and well-put together you are as a person.

- **Never bully yourself:** It's remarkably saddening to think of the emotional and mental abuse we put ourselves through when we allow negative self-talk to govern over our beliefs and actions. Everyone has the inner voice which has an inventory of all the past experiences stored up in your subconscious. That voice uses your memory of those experiences as a weapon to demoralize and discourage you from stepping forward and embracing a better version of yourself and your life today. We feel repulsive when we hear someone emotionally and verbally abusing another person. However, we seldom stop to think about how much we make ourselves suffer by allowing negative voices to keep screaming in our heads and bombarding us with all sorts of fears. This can be considered bullying. That phenomenon has to be changed; it does not naturally just stop. It requires you to be very intentional about silencing that voice and reframing your mind in a way that allows a healthier and more empowering voice to start prevailing. To do so, you have to consider doing a practice called *thought-stopping*. This is when you catch yourself thinking or ruminating on negative things and then immediately short-circuit that thought process. By continually interrupting that thought through mentally changing the subject or redirecting your focus toward more empowering thoughts, you train your mind to start operating in a more positive light. When we don't stop our negative thoughts from running wild, all they will end up doing is dominating us until it becomes impossible to still feel and act confident.

- **Always maintain a positive attitude in both good and bad times:** We have established that true confidence cannot just be limited to the times when you feel like you accomplished many things. It also has to prevail even during times when you feel like you are hitting rock bottom and things aren't going well. Naturally, when things aren't going well, it's easy to plunge into a negative state and immediately your physiology would also start to show signs of your sinking confidence. To ensure that you maintain your confidence, you now have to practice taking more control of your state when dark clouds are looming in your life. Imagine how impressive and astounding it is to still see someone being positive and level-headed when things aren't okay. It's such an attractive quality that makes you very charismatic to the people around you because no one wants to deal with grumpy and moody attitudes. Wallowing in self-pity, complaints, and negative words should no longer be part of your habits and ways. Instead, whenever doors close, always take it as a chance to look for that window you never got to use and enjoy the view! Positive mantras and deepening yourself in mindset training for resilience and success will help to guide you on knowing better ways to respond to life. As you practice showing up with positivity at all times, your self-love and self-respect will also start to flourish because sometimes what makes us despise ourselves are the negative states we often find ourselves in. Many doors open to people who are positive. When you are cynical, chances are you wouldn't be able to view opportunities as opportunities but you would see them as threats instead and end up not doing things that can help you grow. Optimism is pure beauty and they that perpetually possess it seldom sink in the depths of despair but always find ways to soar.

- **Respect your time:** Time is one of the most important resources you will ever have. Learning to manage it effectively will help you have confidence in your timely decision-making. There is an appropriate and best time for doing all the various things life presents to you. Learning to discern the best time for doing things and wholeheartedly devoting your effort toward fully forcing and giving your best in completing what you have to do helps you to produce quality results in your endeavors. An area we all have to be mindful of embracing confidence in is fully enjoying the different times and seasons of our lives. For instance, when you are in elementary school, high school, college, and post-college, you have to be confident to embrace and be fully immersed in that period of your life. Childhood only lasts for a few years, and so does high school and college. Wouldn't it be sad to have very few joyful experiences you can recall from those various stages of your life? Usually, many people tend to realize when it's already too late that they should have been more present during their high school days and enjoyed that stage of their lives. Many people who skip being fully present and open to confidently venture into the adventures those seasons present end up facing a middle-life crisis or wishing they had celebrated their lives before. Think about the attitude you have been having toward the different stages of your life up until now. Would you say that you are proud of how you confidently embraced your childhood, teenagehood, adulthood, or old age? Confidence should not just be limited to a time when your beauty is supposedly at its prime, such as your 20s. No, you are beautiful at every stage of your life. If you reject and convince yourself that you aren't beautiful and worth enjoying every stage of your life, then that would be such an unfortunate way of losing so much valuable time over negative beliefs. When we love and embrace ourselves at every point of our lives, we start fully living meaningful lives filled with fond memories and adventures.

- Do you ever feel like you postpone your happiness and always hesitate to confidently enjoy where you are now? If you do, that's a sign that now it's time to change that for good. Whether it's motherhood, being a sister, being a friend, a work colleague, a romantic partner, or any profession you have now... remember that that's your life presently and you deserve to confidently embrace and celebrate that stage of your life! Living with that positive frame of mind that is conscious of time helps you to live with regrets, knowing that you lived and you will continue to confidently live, laugh, and love no matter what! no longer Don't postpone your happiness to a time when you assume you deserve to be happy. Even if that time comes, you will still feel like it's not yet the right time, and before you know it, years of your life would have been wasted away in deferring your potential to confidently enjoy your time. Start today! Respect now, and think about your attitude toward each day of your life moving forward. Do you try your best to confidently create a beautiful and memorable life for yourself? If not, here comes the chance for you to unlock the door to living that enriched life.

- **Accept worthwhile challenges:** You know that feeling of shock and pleasant surprise when you finally accomplish something you previously thought was out of your league? Isn't it such an elating feeling that leaves you filled with thoughts of all the possible things you can also achieve if only you keep believing in yourself? Confidence has the principle of accepting and not shunning away worthwhile challenges. Instead of saying they can't do something, they choose to focus on finding ways to complete the task. This entails not being afraid to expose your ignorance and ask for help. When we are not feeling confident about something we tend to resist change and fight for things to remain the same. The prospect of change frightens us and makes us uncomfortable because we won't have certainty yet about being competent enough to successfully win the challenges. Confident people do not hide behind myriad concocted excuses of why they can't do something. Instead, they take on worthwhile challenges with the belief that if they search for answers hard enough they will sail through. Such is the kind of powerful mindset we all ought to have if we are to embody ferocious confidence. It is when we allow ourselves to feel uncomfortable and challenged that we give ourselves the chance to discover stronger and much more powerful sides of who we are that we may have been oblivious to. Fall in love with the idea of always escaping the ordinary and reaching out for greater dimensions in your life through trying new things. Confident people are not afraid of depending on others for help and guidance when it's healthy and right for them to seek assistance. They acknowledge and confidently leverage other people's strengths instead of trying to be *a know-it-all person*. By respecting diversity and allowing others to help them, they continue to grow beyond their skill and intelligence level because of being constantly exposed to the nourishing and enlightening ideas and skills of other people more competent in various areas. Don't be afraid to ask for help; doing so is the hallmark of true wisdom and humility.

- **Prioritize self-care:** When we don't neglect ourselves, we are able to sustain positive states for a long time. However, if we neglect to look after ourselves well, our confidence can be shattered at any point in time due to suddenly facing mental or emotional breakdowns or facing failures that leave us feeling doubtful of our abilities. Looking after yourself should never be something that is sidelined because just like anything else that's not well looked after, its performance gradually starts to deteriorate. We are very good at taking great care of our physical possessions. We wash them almost daily, charge our phones daily to restore their power, and do a great job looking after other people. However, sometimes many people just tend to fall into the pattern of being complacent about truly looking after themselves the way they ought to. For instance, if you feel like you keep battling with intrusive negative thoughts that bring you down and childhood trauma, the idea of investing in working through those issues with a professional therapist might be looked down upon. However, it's actually what could help you to finally break free from thought patterns and beliefs entrenched in you that would only fade away if you put in intensive work to fight them. Whether you are doing well or not, working with a therapist is always a great way to look after yourself.

- There is the stereotype that therapists are only meant for people who think they are broken and damaged. However, this is just a narrow-minded way of understanding the benefits you can accrue from investing in that form of self-care. By working with a therapist, your mind starts to be open to understanding many things about human behavior that you may have never known on your own. This understanding will equip you to manage yourself and others better so that you can continue to show up as the confident version of yourself. You can also learn better ways to manage conflict, be it resolving past disputes or being equipped to handle future misunderstandings in a way that is noble and effective. This will bulletproof your mental health and help you to be more grounded in your values as an individual. Besides seeing a therapist, there are many other ways you can continue to maintain your confidence such as meditating, journaling, and keeping images that show the road map of your confidence journey—this will remind you how far you came up until now and give you the courage and assurance you need that you can do anything you resolve to do.

- Now that we know of the principles that will help you to ground your confidence, let's explore ways you can employ the growth mindset in ensuring that you will continue to progress in your confidence journey until you reach your fullest potential.

The Benefits of Self-Reflection and Evaluation

Self-evaluation is the answer to gaining perspective of where you are coming from, where you are, and where you want to go. When you evaluate yourself, it helps you to see what's working and what's not. It also helps you to notice what needs to be improved and what you need help with. There is no set time rigidly meant to be the only time for self-evaluation, it's a practice you can decide when to take depending on your goals. Generally, it's always good to evaluate your days and also have time to check your weekly and monthly performance. This will help you to not continue to do things that may be jeopardizing your success. It will also help you to set higher goals for yourself so that you don't continue being comfortable with the same level of success. Time moves so fast and that is why we have to be careful to take time to introspect our lives and check if we are still heading toward the right direction and destination we intend to go.

Here are some of the notable benefits of regular self-evaluation:

- It enlightens you about your strengths and weaknesses, and this helps you to put in place strategies to overcome the weaknesses and amplify or harness your strengths more.

- It helps you to appreciate your efforts more and celebrate your progress.

- It helps you to know how to improve your emotional intelligence and work better with others.

- It encourages strategic and creative thinking, which is helpful for problem-solving and fostering excellence performance.

- It helps in restoring momentum and renewing your motivation.

- Provides room for constructive feedback, leading to better systems and strategies put in place to generate better results.

- It boosts your confidence!

People who are constantly thinking of ways to grow often attract abundant success into their lives at such an astounding rate. If you are indeed tired of settling for less and living a shallow life way below your true potential, now is the time to embrace change and start showing up as the person you have always wanted to be. All you have to do now is make up your mind and always decide to be who you want to be. Remember that power is in your hands, so never be afraid to use it anymore, for fear is now merely ancient history!

OTHER BOOK BY AUTHOR

"Stop Overthinking and Get Your Act together"

https://www.amazon.com/dp/B0C7TTYCYQ

Conclusion

Up until now, you have spent countless nights and days longing for the day you will finally start to live your best life. Your burning desire for a better and more fulfilling way of living your life has led you to learn so many things over all these years you have been on planet Earth. Everything you went through was certainly for a greater purpose. Now the time has come for you to harness all that wisdom you have accumulated over all the years of your life so far. Now is the time to start using all these life lessons as tools to build that life you keep dreaming about and seeing in your imagination. No, you are not delusional for believing that you were created for soaring and living a tremendously successful life with unstoppable confidence. What you saw in your heart is exactly what's meant to be and even more. Now the day has dawned for you to no longer keep dreaming but to wake up and manifest those dreams in your real life. You have all it takes to succeed in this quest. Once you focus on winning one day at a time, as you glance back someday, you will be in awe of the beautifully magnificent life you would have created for yourself.

Gone are the days of being a victim of your past painful experiences. Gone are those ancient days of living below your potential. Enough is enough, what is left for you now is to embrace your inside-out beauty and unapologetically live your best life. The power to make all those changes rests with you. Every time you feel low or find yourself in doubt, remember that all that is just temporary and it does not define who you are. You are someone uniquely created for an extraordinary life of tremendous and perpetual growth and success.

Remember that the more you keep showing up as the person you want to be, the more your brain will be undergoing cognitive restructuring. This means that as you adopt confident habits, an entirely new neurological network is established in your brain which enables you to start performing those habits automatically without having to use much of your conscious decision-making power. Once you reach that stage, you would know that indeed a revolution has occurred, and never again will you ever be the old version of yourself. All you need to do to get there is to maintain consistency as much as possible. You will face many challenges, some days you will feel like giving up, and some days you won't feel confident; all that is part of the process. What matters is that you commit to rising up again and moving forward no matter what. Before you know it, your entire life would have started to transform and be filled with undeniable and heart-moving success stories of your confidence journey. YOU have all it takes to make it, believe in this infallible truth today, tomorrow, and forever.

I congratulate you for taking on this journey! You deserve to celebrate this huge milestone of how far you have come up until now. I look forward to reading your reviews on **"How To Build Unstoppable Confidence Within Yourself"** on Amazon and hearing about your success stories.

It's truly incredible to witness your dedication to personal development and the desire to unlock your true potential. As you jump on this journey of confidence building, I wanted to share something special with you.

I invite you to explore another valuable resource that complements your current reading experience. I have another resource here that I know is of great value that you can also dive into, **"Stop Overthinking and Get Your Act Together."**

This book provides beneficial tools for personal development, self-improvement, and mindfulness practices. You will gain a better understanding of the nature of overthinking and how it affects their lives. You can also learn practical strategies for overcoming negative thought patterns and managing your thoughts and emotions more effectively.

I hope to inspire you to approach life's challenges with a sense of curiosity and openness, and to develop a growth mindset that allows you to embrace change and pursue your goals with confidence.

I honestly believe that by understanding and conquering overthinking, you'll strengthen the very foundation of your confidence, paving the way for a life of empowerment and success.

Investing in your personal development is a powerful choice. So, why not seize this opportunity to explore both books and unlock the extraordinary within you?

Enjoy a boundless confidence and fulfilling life.

May you live the rest of your life always having faith and unwavering confidence in yourself; you are indeed an absolute treasure and nothing can change that.

About the Author

Lara J. Noble is a pharmacist by profession. She is a mom of four beautiful children and is currently living in Northern California, USA. She has always had a deep love for nature and enjoys spending time outdoors, hiking, and exploring the beauty of the natural world. Lara is also an accomplished writer, with a passion for self-help, motivational, and inspirational books. She is passionate about helping people escape the confines of living lives below their fullest potential. Through this book on confidence, she hopes to motivate and equip readers to be confident and overcome the limiting beliefs and fears that hold them back from having faith in their unique abilities.

Through confidence, you can embrace your true identity and enjoy living a life filled with adventure and continuous growth. Confidence comes from within, there is no reason to wait any longer. Lara's hope is to help people to start living the lives they deserve instead of being controlled by false beliefs and crippling habits. The answer to unlocking the door of this new reality is fully embodying confidence and courageously going after the life of your dreams.

References

Aberin, D. (2022, June 29). *40 Quotes About Celebrating Your Inner Beauty*. The Gambler. https://thegaggler.com/40-powerful-quotes-to-celebrate-your-inner-beauty/

Ackerman, C. (2019, July 3). *What is Self-Confidence? + 9 Ways to Increase It [2019 Update]*. PositivePsychology.com. https://positivepsychology.com/self-confidence/

Arruda, G. (2021, February 24). *How to Improve your style in 10 easy steps*. Gabriella Arruda. https://gabriellearruda.com/how-to-improve-your-style-in-10-easy-steps/

Austin, A. (2018, June 6). *The Relationship Between Gratitude & Confidence*. Poised & Professional - Coaching with Alyssa Austin. https://poisedandprofessional.com/2018/06/why-gratitude-is-the-key-to-becoming-more-confident/

Australia, H. (2022, October 19). *Motivation: How to get started and staying motivated*. Www.healthdirect.gov.au. https://www.healthdirect.gov.au/motivation-how-to-get-started-and-staying-motivated#:~:text=Remember%20why%20you%20wanted%20to

Barclay, T. (2021, October 25). *How Does Physical Appearance Affect Self-Esteem?* Innerbody. https://www.innerbody.com/relationship-between-body-image-and-self-esteem

Boswell, R. (2022, April 12). *Why is Self Confidence Important to Success | Rachel Boswell*. Rachel Boswell Coaching.

https://rachel-boswell.com/why-is-self-confidence-important-to-success/

Brosix . (2022, May 10). *60 Communication Quotes Highlighting The Importance - Brosix.* Brosix Blog. https://www.brosix.com/blog/communication-quotes/

Brown, L. (2022). *What Is Effective Communication?* Laurie Brown Communications. https://lauriebrown.com/guides/communication-skills/what-is-effective-communication/

Cherry, K. (2021, June 22). *Common Signs of Low Self-Esteem.* Verywell Mind. https://www.verywellmind.com/signs-of-low-self-esteem-5185978

Collins, C. (2020, April 21). *The Importance of Self Confidence for Your Success.* Mom's Got Money. https://www.momsgotmoney.com/the-importance-of-self-confidence/

Cover, S. (2020, July 30). *The 4 Elements To Confidence.* Social. https://socialifestylemag.com/2020/07/the-4-elements-to-confidence/

Davenport, B. (2022, November 21). *How To Always Be Authentic And Stay True To Yourself.* Live Bold and Bloom. https://liveboldandbloom.com/11/self-confidence/be-true-to-yourself

Edwards, V. V. (2022, July 26). *How to Fix Your Posture (in Just 5 Minutes or Less!).* Science of People. https://www.scienceofpeople.com/confident-posture/

Erieau, C. (2019, February 20). *The 50 Best Resilience Quotes - Driven.* Driven App.

https://home.hellodriven.com/articles/the-50-best-resilience-quotes/

Estrada, J. (2020, October 25). *6 Ways to Practice Positive Self-Talk To Improve Self Esteem.* Well+Good. https://www.wellandgood.com/positive-self-talk/

Fran. (2022, April 25). *What is a growth mindset and how can you develop one?* FutureLearn. https://www.futurelearn.com/info/blog/general/develop-growth-mindset

Gitnux. (2023, March 23). *The Most Surprising Self Confidence Statistics And Trends in [year] • GITNUX.* Gitnuxblog. https://blog.gitnux.com/self-confidence-statistics/

Guagliardo, R. (2018, March 29). *Council Post: Overcoming Fear And Achieving Your Goals Starts With One Simple Step.* Forbes. https://www.forbes.com/sites/forbescoachescouncil/2018/03 /29/overcoming-fear-and-achieving-your-goals-starts-with-one-simple-step/?sh=8fc831303da1

Habash, C. (2022, February 1). *What is self-reflection, and why is it important for self-improvement? - Thriveworks.* Counseling and Life Coaching - Find a Counselor. https://thriveworks.com/blog/importance-self-reflection-improvement/

Half, R. (2015, July 15). *12 Quotes to Inspire Confidence at Work.* Www.roberthalf.com. https://www.roberthalf.com/blog/management-tips/12-quotes-to-inspire-confidence-at-work

Hall, L. (2022, February 25). *Boost Your Confidence with These Uplifting Quotes.* Country Living.

https://www.countryliving.com/life/inspirational-stories/a39116740/confidence-quotes/

Hope+wellness. (2019, January 28). *18 Quotes to Inspire Self-Kindness and Self-Compassion.* Hope+Wellness. https://www.hope-wellness.com/blog/18-quotes-to-inspire-self-kindness-and-self-compassion#:~:text=%E2%80%9CIf%20your%20compassion%20does%20not

Lancer, D. (2016, February 28). *Self-Esteem Makes Successful Relationships.* Psych Central. https://psychcentral.com/lib/self-esteem-makes-successful-relationships

Lowenbraun, N. (2020, August 5). *6 Key Facts About Facial Expressions When Presenting.* Duarte. https://www.duarte.com/facial-expressions-matter-when-presenting-heres-why/

Marcus, B. (2017, October 17). *How Does A Lack Of Confidence Affect Your Life And Career?* Forbes. https://www.forbes.com/sites/bonniemarcus/2017/10/17/how-does-a-lack-of-confidence-affect-your-life-and-career/?sh=142da7b71ac4

Marinoff, E. (2020a, March 11). *How to Define Your Personal Values and Live By Them.* Lifehack. https://www.lifehack.org/866227/personal-values#1-personal-values-help-with-self-awareness

Marinoff, E. (2020b, March 11). *How to define your personal values and live by them for a fulfilling life.* Lifehack. https://www.lifehack.org/866227/personal-values

Marketing. (2022, January 17). *Confidence & Relationships: Why Is It Important?* PIVOT. https://www.lovetopivot.com/why-confidence-important-build-relationship-coaching-online/

Michael, J. (2016, August 22). *How to Identify Your Strengths and Weaknesses -*. Bplans Blog. https://articles.bplans.com/how-to-identify-your-strengths-and-weaknesses/

Oregon Counseling. (2022, November 17). *Gratitude And Mental Health.* Oregon Counseling. https://oregoncounseling.com/article/gratitude-and-mental-health/

Pangilinan, J. (2022, January 10). *133 Positivity Quotes to Keep You Motivated During Challenges.* Happier Human. https://www.happierhuman.com/positivity-qoutes/

Parker, L. (2023, February 23). *How to advocate for yourself at work.* Work Life by Atlassian. https://www.atlassian.com/blog/productivity/advocating-for-yourself-at-work

Perry, E. (2022, July 27). *The Meaning of Personal Values: How They Shape Your Life.* Www.betterup.com. https://www.betterup.com/blog/meaning-of-personal-values

Psychology Today. (2019). *Confidence | Psychology Today.* Psychology Today. https://www.psychologytoday.com/us/basics/confidence

Robbins, T. (2019). *How to Be Confident, 3 Easy Tips to Transform Your Confidence Today.* Tonyrobbins.com. https://www.tonyrobbins.com/building-confidence/how-to-be-confident/

Ronin, K. (2020, June 19). *9 Myths About Confidence That Are Holding You Back.* The Muse.

https://www.themuse.com/advice/9-myths-about-confidence-that-are-holding-you-back

Selig, M. (2018, August 22). *10 Myths About Confidence That Are Holding You Back | Psychology Today.* Www.psychologytoday.com. https://www.psychologytoday.com/us/blog/changepower/20 1808/10-myths-about-confidence-are-holding-you-back

Simon. (2013, April 15). *Why what we value defines our personal identity.* The Right Questions. https://therightquestions.co/why-what-we-value-defines-our-personal-identity/

Smith, S. (2021, January 11). *20 Benefits of Healthy Relationships.* Marriage Advice - Expert Marriage Tips & Advice. https://www.marriage.com/advice/relationship/benefits-of-healthy-relationships/

Sood, A. (2022, July 11). *Top Tips to Help You Build and Cultivate Resilience.* EverydayHealth.com. https://www.everydayhealth.com/wellness/resilience/top-tips-help-build-cultivate-resilience

Sparks, R. (2019, August 12). *Council Post: Three Key Ingredients For Authentic Self-Confidence.* Forbes. https://www.forbes.com/sites/forbescoachescouncil/2019/08 /12/three-key-ingredients-for-authentic-self-confidence/?sh=3173add3507d

Tesema, M. (2020, July 29). *Here Are the 3 Elements to Building a Foundation of Self-Confidence.* Shine. https://advice.theshineapp.com/articles/here-are-the-3-elements-to-building-a-foundation-of-self-confidence/

Thompson, M. (2021, May 11). *The Benefits of Self Evaluation and Assessment*. WeThrive. https://wethrive.net/blog/self-evaluation-and-assessment/

Umlas, R. (2023, January 4). *Embrace your quirks: 10 reasons why being unique is a good thing*. Hack Spirit. https://hackspirit.com/why-being-unique-is-a-good-thing/

Virginia Department of health. (2021). *Self-Acceptance – Workforce Wellness*. Virginia.gov. https://www.vdh.virginia.gov/workforce-wellness/wellness-topics/self-acceptance/

Waters, S. (2022, April 13). *Healthy Boundaries in Relationships: A Guide for Building and Keeping*. Www.betterup.com. https://www.betterup.com/blog/healthy-boundaries-in-relationships

Whitney, D. (2020, October 13). *Self-Acceptance: How to Embrace and Love Yourself Unconditionally (When The World Tells You Not To)*. Whitney Gordon-Mead. https://whitneygordon-mead.com/2020/10/13/self-acceptance-how-to-embrace-and-love-yourself-unconditionally-when-the-world-tells-you-not-to/

Wilding, M. J. (2017, May 10). *5 Different Types of Imposter Syndrome (and 5 Ways to Battle Each One)*. Themuse.com; The Muse. https://www.themuse.com/advice/5-different-types-of-imposter-syndrome-and-5-ways-to-battle-each-one

Williams, D. (2017, May 29). *7 Types of Obstacles You May Face*. Dave Williams Ministries. https://davewilliams.com/types-of-obstacles/

Wright, S. (2020, August 20). *Developing Resilience and Perseverance - Everyone Active*. Everyone Active.

https://www.everyoneactive.com/content-hub/home-workouts/developing-resilience-and-perseverance/

.

Made in the USA
Las Vegas, NV
04 October 2023

78551519R00089